From Veil to Valor

Unveiling Your Authentic Self

Stephanie B Martin

Dedication

To all who struggle to shine their inner light beneath their daily mask, this book is for you! May you learn to love yourself truly and trust that you are designed exactly as God intended. May you find strength in your vulnerabilities, courage in your doubts, and joy in your journey. Remember, you are never alone on this path. May the words on the pages inspire you to believe in yourself, uplift you to aim for higher, and encourage you to find your valor!

Acknowledgments

To God, I give all the honor, glory, and gratitude for this life He has bestowed upon me!

To my husband, Tuboris, the best friend and life partner I could have, thank you for always loving me completely, seeing me for who I am, and allowing me to pursue all my heart desires. My heart beats in rhythm with yours!

To my children, DeJanae, Jurieen, and Tesia, who continue to make me proud and give me reasons to excel. You are three of my greatest achievements in life, and I love you unconditionally!

To my mother and her unconditional love and belief in me. Thank you for always making me feel that I could accomplish anything.

Lastly, to my dear friend Sharolyn Payton, whom I truly miss, thank you for always seeing the light in me.

Contents

Introduction: The Journey Within

The journey toward self-discovery and strength involves embracing vulnerability, a step many might find daunting. It's like standing at the edge of a cliff, preparing to dive into the unknown depths below—scary, yes, but also where the magic of growth begins. This insight echoes the wisdom of the proverb, *"Only when we are brave enough to explore the darkness will we discover the infinite power of our light."*

The adventure kicked off during a chaotic period of my life where all the jigsaw pieces of my puzzled existence were scattered without discernible order or meaning. Each fragment - my relationships, career aspirations, self-worth, hopes, and dreams - seemed entirely unconnected, leaving me bewildered as to how or where to even start making sense of it all. The concept of vulnerability first entered my awareness amidst this tempest of turmoil and confusion. My initial reaction, like many others, was to deem it as a sign of weakness, an Achilles heel best kept hidden away and protected. Yet, as I continued stumbling through the disorderliness enveloping my world, my perspective on vulnerability began to shift subtly.

I came to understand that vulnerability was not a character flaw but rather a display of inner fortitude - the resolve to unflinchingly confront myself, acknowledge my deepest uncertainties and insecurities, and discard the façade I had long put into view externally. It required relinquishing superficial masks and facing my authentic self in all its imperfections. This enlightenment did not come easily; instead, it emerged through many sleepless nights of introspection, private journaling of thoughts and sentiments, and opening up to others in unprecedented ways. A pivotal moment in this path of self-discovery arrived when I decided to seek help actively. Though a simple decision, it proved profoundly impactful, marking the inception of a process akin to an inward dig of my very psyche.

With guidance, I started peeling back layer upon layer to uncover the roots of fears and doubts long buried beneath my subconscious. This process was far from comfortable, akin to weathering a storm and fully experiencing each raindrop and gust. Yet, facing such trials proved imperative for growth.

As I delved deeper into exploring my insecurities, I began to recognize the inner strength that lies in being honest about weakness. It's paradoxical, truly. You'd think laying bare your fragile core to the world would make you more prone to pain, but in actuality, it achieves the opposite. It cultivates resilience. Each time I confronted a fear, shared an imperfection, or voiced a doubt, I was essentially strengthening my intrinsic grit. It was as if every confession of vulnerability was contributing to a fortress, and with each addition, I was building walls around my heart, not to exclude others but to shield my newly found strength.

This transformation didn't happen overnight. It was a gradual process, filled with setbacks and victories. There were moments of doubt, where the old fears threatened to resurface, whispering that I was not enough, that I was unworthy.

But with each of these moments, I found a little more fight within me. I began to challenge these negative voices, to question their validity, and, in doing so, I discovered my true strength. This strength wasn't about being invincible or fearless.

It was about comprehending that I could face whatever life presented and emerge on the other side, maybe a little battered but never broken. It was about understanding that my vulnerabilities were not defects but rather aspects of my humanity, foundations of empathy, and connection with others.

Sharing my account, my journey through vulnerability to strength is not just recounting my personal evolution. It's providing a beacon of hope to others who may be standing on their own cliffs, reluctant to plunge into the depths of their being. It's about acknowledging, "Yes, it's scary. Yes, it's difficult. But it's also worthwhile."

This expedition has reshaped my perspective on life, relationships, and myself. It has taught me the value of genuine connections, the kind that can only be forged when we dare to be open and vulnerable. It has demonstrated to me that bravery in the face of adversity defines strength, not how effectively we face our challenges. Perhaps most importantly, it has shown us that transformation is about unveiling our true selves, not just about changing who we are.

In reflecting on this path, I'm reminded that accepting vulnerability is only the start of a voyage that will go forth. It lays the groundwork for a lifetime of personal development, pushing beyond our comfort zones and discovering not only our strength but also our warmth, compassion, and limitless potential. Therefore, those who are on the verge of something new should know that despite the fear that comes with taking a giant leap, the journey from weakness to strength is one of the most rewarding experiences one can have.

Shedding the Veil

Imagine each of us wearing an invisible cloak from the day we start understanding the world around us. All of the roles, expectations, and rules that society assigns us—including what we should achieve and how we should behave—combine to form this cloak. It's heavy, isn't it? This cloak, which I refer to as the "veil," conceals our true selves and smothers the individualities, dreams, and ideals that make us who we are. It's like walking through life in a costume that never quite fits, constantly adjusting it in hopes of finding comfort that never comes.

This veil does more than just conceal; it distorts. It filters how we see ourselves and how we think we should be seen by others. It's similar to seeing our actual reflection obscured by dust and dirt in a mirror. We get a peek at our potential selves, but those are brief moments that are sometimes overshadowed by the demands of the next set of expectations.

However, here lies the magnificent part: there exists a way to shed this veil, wipe the dirt from the mirror, lighten the load, and let our real selves not just breathe but shine brightly. It doesn't demand grand gestures or seismic shifts in our everyday lives. Rather, it's found in small, honest moments alone with ourselves—questioning, "Is this truly what I want, or am I striving to fit someone else's idea of who I should be?"

The path to removing the veil and forging a deeper connection with our spiritual selves is straightforward at its heart. It calls for moments of silence, where the only voice you heed is your own, not muffled by the clamor of the world. It champions vulnerability, urging you to show your true colors to the world despite fearing judgment. It speaks of finding a bond with something greater, whatever that may signify to you, as a reminder that we are part of a vast, interconnected tapestry.

And if there's one nugget of wisdom to hold onto, it's this: *"Being yourself is the loveliest thing you can be."* Consider this for a moment. Amid the myriad roles we play—whether as professionals climbing the career ladder, parents nurturing a family, students striving for academic excellence, or friends offering unwavering support—and the weighty expectations we shoulder, just being ourselves—unfiltered, unvarnished, undeniably us—is the most authentic and beautiful contribution we can make to the world.

Each role comes with its own script, a set of lines we're expected to deliver perfectly. The professional must exude confidence and ambition; the parent must be endlessly patient and wise; the student must forever be curious and diligent; and the friend must always be available and understanding.

Yet, within each of us, there are many facets that these roles can neither contain nor define. There's the dreamer who gazes at the stars, the adventurer yearning for uncharted paths, the creator with a soul aching to express itself, and the quiet observer finding wonder in the simplest of moments.

It's in these spaces between roles, in the quiet aftermath of fulfilled expectations, where our true selves whisper to us. Shedding the veil means listening to these whispers, allowing them to guide us toward a life where we're not just performing roles but living authentically, driven by our genuine desires and passions. The main goal of this book is to help readers surmount self-doubt and develop a stronger bond with their spiritual essence. It's common to feel lost beneath the weight of social expectations, which can lead to a fog of uncertainty about our own worth and purpose. This book acts as a light, leading readers through the haze of self-doubt toward a place of self-assurance and spiritual insight.

Through its pages, the book emphasizes the importance of recognizing and letting go of the doubts that hold us back.

It motivates readers to consider significant questions about their aspirations and ambitions, liberated from the sway of outside forces. The process outlined in the book focuses not on drastic gestures but on embracing small, honest moments revealing our true selves and wants.

In addition, the guide emphasizes the necessity of reflection and the courage to reveal our genuine selves to others, even when facing potential disapproval. It highlights the importance of staying spiritually connected, reminding us of our interrelated collective role within a world much larger than our desires and wants.

The book's ultimate message is simple yet profound: embracing and expressing our true nature is not just liberating; it's the most genuine form of beauty we can offer. *"The privilege of a lifetime is to become who you truly are."* This sentiment captures the essence of the book's aim, encouraging a journey not just of self-discovery but of self-acceptance and expression.

The Spiritual Path to Authentic Living

Understanding the importance of the spiritual journey in attaining an authentic existence resembles undertaking a profound, individual quest. This expedition is about connecting with the core of your identity, stripping away the expectations of society and personal insecurities. It invites you on an introspective journey to uncover and accept your real identity, unburdened by the forces that have molded your sense of self.

Engaging with your spiritual identity isn't limited to times of reflection or isolation; it's a constant conversation with your innermost thoughts and emotions. It involves posing challenging questions to yourself: What gives me happiness? What are my core principles? How do I perceive meaning and satisfaction? And, importantly, does my lifestyle reflect these truths? This endeavor isn't focused on reaching conclusive solutions. Rather, it emphasizes becoming at ease with questioning and seeking, allowing your spiritual realizations to shape your decisions and conduct.

One might wonder why this spiritual exploration is vital to living authentically. The reason is simple: Without knowing who we are at our core, our lives can easily become reflections of others' expectations instead of our own.

We might find ourselves distracted by goals that leave us unfulfilled or wearing masks that don't fit our true faces. In contrast, embracing our spiritual selves empowers authentic living. Our decisions stem from inner knowing rather than following crowds. This doesn't mean the route is straightforward. It takes courage to face ourselves with honesty, acknowledging fears and dreams alike. It demands resilience to walk roads less traveled. But the rewards of such courage are limitless: a life of authenticity where every choice is a reflection of our true selves.

Moreover, this spiritual work cultivates compassion extending beyond individual experiences. As we learn ourselves, we understand others better. We see shared hopes in different skins. This empathy strengthens bonds built on mutual care and insight. It also nourishes our sense of place in the world. By aligning lives with spiritual truths, we contribute to a collective energy valuing sincerity, kindness, and integrity.

In essence, unveiling and welcoming our authentic selves is challenging and rewarding, urging us to face our insecurities and apprehensions while offering a more authentic, fulfilling life. This path of self-realization and acceptance of our spiritual selves does not end at a specific milestone but symbolizes an ongoing exploration of personal development and insight. It prompts us to lead purposeful lives directed by our core beliefs and principles and to build relationships based on authenticity and mutual respect.

Chapter 1: Shedding the Veil - Embracing Authenticity in Everyday Life

In the bustling journey of life, individuals often find themselves juggling a variety of roles, each carrying its own set of expectations that influence both their personal and professional spheres. This dynamic can enrich life but also presents challenges in balancing demands. The complexity of managing these various aspects has significant repercussions on an individual's well-being, relationships, and career progression.

In the personal realm, individuals take on various roles such as parent, partner, sibling, child, and friend, each with its unique set of expectations and duties. For instance, parents are tasked with providing nurture, guidance, and support to their children, a role that requires patience, a significant investment of time, and emotional engagement. Beyond meeting a child's bodily needs, this caring embraces their emotional and intellectual development and creates a safe and nurturing environment for their growth. Couples or spouses are expected to support one another, share life's hardships, and keep a loving relationship. This partnership often involves navigating life's ups and downs together, forging stronger bonds through mutual understanding and shared experiences.

People may find themselves extensively involved in the care of their elderly parents as youngsters or even as adults, providing support and assistance as needed. The parent-child bond gains a new depth as a result of this role reversal, which emphasizes appreciation and respect for the years of care given. Friendships require commitment, regard for one another, and emotional support. Different from family ties, these relationships provide a special kind of support that makes life more enjoyable by bringing companionship, understanding, and shared joys. Playing these roles helps to create a network of emotional support that is essential for conquering obstacles and enjoying life's victories.

These expectations shape how people behave and make decisions and ultimately affect relationships by influencing how they engage with each other in their personal circles. The fulfillment of these roles adds to the web of knowledge and assistance that supports wholesome interpersonal interactions and individual well-being. *'We are what we repeatedly do. Excellence, then, is not an act, but a habit,'* as Aristotle once stated, considering the significance of role fulfillment and how it affects personal growth.

Effectively navigating these positions fosters human development and imparts valuable lessons about love, empathy, and perseverance. Additionally, it fortifies the bonds of mutual respect and compassion, strengthening the fabric of society. Even though it's difficult, maintaining these kinds of deep, meaningful ties that improve people's lives requires this delicate balancing act. Indeed, it is through the diligent embrace of these roles and the lessons they impart that we carve our paths toward a richer, more connected existence.

It takes knowledge of other people's needs and expectations, as well as a willingness to meet those needs, to engage in these roles successfully. It also entails having a profound appreciation for these relationships and realizing the value they bring to life. This knowledge is developed from experiences and introspection on the nature of these relationships rather than being intrinsic.

Because of the love and support of their personal relationships, each person may flourish in this caring setting. Furthermore, it fosters a culture of giving and receiving in which everyone benefits from strong emotional bonds.

As one moves into the professional world, the range of responsibilities increases and includes jobs as an employee, manager, business owner, and mentor. As workers, people have responsibilities that include fulfilling job requirements, supporting the team in accomplishing goals, and following business policies.

This position demands devotion to the company's vision, teamwork skills, and determination. Managers or supervisors are responsible for guiding their teams, making strategic choices that affect the course of projects, and supporting their team members' professional growth. Strong decision-making abilities, an awareness of team dynamics, and a dedication to developing talent inside the company are demands for this leadership position.

Entrepreneurs lead their ventures, navigate decision-making paths, welcome challenges, and cultivate new ideas, all while meeting the expectations of those invested in their projects. This journey demands a distinct combination of foresight, bravery, and tenacity as they transform ideas into successful enterprises.

They must continually adapt to market shifts, predict future patterns, and allocate resources wisely to guarantee the endurance and expansion of their businesses. Conversely, mentors commit to directing their mentees toward personal and career growth, imparting their wisdom, experiences, and understanding. This bond benefits the mentee and provides the mentor with novel viewpoints and the gratification of aiding in another's development. Each role within the professional realm presents its specific obstacles and benefits. By dedicating their capabilities and diligence to shared objectives, workers establish the foundation for the company's achievements.

Their contribution is vital to the practical implementation of business tactics, demanding them to be versatile, dependable, and skilled in their specialties. Supervisors and managers connect the staff and senior management, guaranteeing that collective efforts align with the company's goals. Their function is critical in fostering an efficient working atmosphere, inspiring staff members, and leading the group toward accomplishments.

In the broader context, these professional roles contribute substantially to the social and economic fabric when taken as a whole. Entrepreneurs are essential to the economy's dynamism because they foster innovation and the development of jobs.

Their journey is also quite personal because their endeavors frequently represent personal passions and goals. Mentors ensure the continuation of knowledge and the advancement of industries by imparting their wisdom to the next generation of experts. Every position, from employee to mentor, represents a vital facet of the working world and emphasizes the connection between individual endeavors and group success.

The interplay between personal and professional roles frequently creates difficult situations where people must set priorities, make choices, and occasionally compromise. These roles' expectations are frequently at odds with one another;

however, they can occasionally coexist peacefully. For example, when family emergencies or childcare demands occur, a parent's position may collide with a professional one. In a similar vein, social commitments and personal relationships may be strained by the long hours of some jobs.

These expectations and roles don't exist in a vacuum; they interrelate with one another. A role's success and fulfillment can boost one's self-esteem and performance in another.

On the other hand, difficulties or setbacks in one area of life might negatively impact other aspects as well. These positions' relative weights fluctuate according to life phases, professional routes, and individual preferences.

For well-being and happiness, it is essential to comprehend and navigate the many responsibilities and expectations in one's personal and professional life.

Every role and expectation adds to the complex fabric of a person's life by impacting their relationships, decisions, and course through life. Mastering these roles—adapting, setting priorities, and finding contentment—is essential to navigating life's complex path.

Practical Tips for Embracing Your True Self

How frequently do we stop to think about the persona we showcase to the outside world? Through life's journey, many adopt a range of disguises, or "masks," to navigate the varied roles in personal, professional, and societal realms. These masks can sometimes shield us, yet more frequently, they obstruct our ability to form real bonds with others and ourselves. Detecting and discarding these covers is essential for leading a life filled with fulfillment and authenticity. Here are practical steps to uncover and embrace your genuine self:

1. Self-Reflection:

Identifying you're utilizing these masks marks the initial phase toward shedding them. Set aside moments for introspection. Employ writing or contemplation to delve into your thoughts, emotions, and conduct. Challenge yourself with questions like, "What parts of my persona do I conceal from view, and for what reasons?" "What concerns me about unveiling my authentic self?" This examination aids in deciphering the concealed aspects of your identity, embarking on a quest to your true essence, and stripping back each layer to uncover your fundamental nature

2. Acknowledge Your Fears:

Masks are frequently adopted out of fear—apprehension of judgment, rejection, or not succeeding. Recognize these fears as a typical aspect of the human condition. By addressing these anxieties head-on, you reduce their influence over you. Realize that all individuals have insecurities and that vulnerability is a forte, not a frailty, capable of fostering more profound connections with others. Accepting these apprehensions as widespread can foster a sense of unity and bravery to confront them directly.

3. Practice Vulnerability:

Start small by confiding in close friends or family members about personal experiences, ideas, or emotions. Choose open, encouraging individuals and safe environments. Although it can be intimidating, practicing vulnerability is essential to becoming honest. Recall that vulnerability fosters closeness and trust in relationships. Your relationships with those around you are strengthened by this openness, which serves as a bridge to real connections.

4. Set Boundaries:

You don't have to be transparent to everyone when you take off your masks. Deciding who gets to see the different aspects of who you really are is the key to setting good boundaries. It's acceptable to be more guarded around some people and more open with others. When deciding when and with whom to share your true self, follow your gut. These boundaries guarantee that your transparency is appreciated and accepted while also safeguarding your mental health.

5. Seek Feedback:

We can be blind to our own masks at times. Therapists, family members, or close friends can provide priceless insights into patterns or behaviors we might not see. Ask these reliable people for their opinions on how you come across in various situations. Instead of using this criticism as judgment, use it as guidance to better understand and modify your behavior. This outside perspective can play a crucial role in identifying and removing the masks you unconsciously wear.

6. Embrace Your Flaws:

Knowing the fact that being imperfect is inherently human, welcome your peculiarities, errors, and shortcomings as they contribute to your distinctiveness. Accepting these imperfections allows others to feel free to express their true selves in your presence, fostering a more genuine and encouraging atmosphere. Appreciating these flaws, instead of concealing them, may result in a profound sense of self-recognition and a collective sense of humanity.

7. Pursue Activities That Align With Your Interests:

Take up interests and pursuits that align with your authentic self. Engaging in hobbies such as sports, music, painting, or any other interest lets your true personality come out. They give you the kind of happiness and contentment that can only be found when you pursue your passions. Giving these interests your whole attention can be a potent way to convey who you are and what you stand for.

8. Monitor Your Social Media Presence:

The representation of an idealized self is frequently encouraged by social media. Consider carefully how you choose to present yourself online. Prioritize sincerity over perfection. To give a more true picture of your life, share authentic moments with others, including the challenges. This promotes more sincere communication with your virtual community. Honest sharing mitigates the constraints of social media perfection by promoting an online community that is more sincere and encouraging.

9. Practice Self-Compassion:

Treat yourself well while you're doing this. Mask removal is difficult and can make you uncomfortable as you face concealed parts of yourself. Practice self-compassion by treating yourself with the same kindness, concern, and support you would offer a good friend. This self-kindness is crucial in navigating the journey of self-discovery and change with patience and understanding.

10. Celebrate Your Progress:

Acknowledge and rejoice in each step you take in the direction of authenticity. These are important turning points in your journey, whether it's confiding in a friend, establishing limits, or accepting a weakness.

To encourage good change, remember to celebrate these occasions. No matter how small, appreciating and acknowledging your accomplishments may be very uplifting and reassuring, promoting ongoing development and authenticity.

Thus, taking off the masks we wear to show who we really are is a brave path that results in a more fulfilled life, richer relationships, and a better understanding of ourselves.

Accepting your true self and letting it show through helps you build relationships based on sincere communication and respect for one another. Never forget that your unique contributions benefit the world; therefore, embrace your individuality.

Cultivating Authenticity through Meditation and Mindfulness

Reflecting on the essence of our true selves, it's evident that the roles and expectations imposed by society can obscure our authenticity. The disciplines of meditation and mindfulness offer a return path to our genuine selves, promoting deep introspection and a reconnection with our fundamental values and convictions. These straightforward exercises are aimed at cultivating authenticity, enabling a life lived with fullness and sincerity, free from societal constraints.

Mindful Breathing for Presence:

Start with the fundamentals of mindful breathing to help you ground yourself in the here and now. Locate a calm area and take a comfortable seat. Close your eyes and inhale deeply and slowly. Pay attention to the feeling of air coming in and going out of your nose. Refocus your attention back to your breathing when your thoughts stray from it. By calming the cacophony of everyday life, this practice facilitates self-connection. It reminds us that we can discover who we really are with just a breath, which promotes serenity and stability in the midst of life's chaos.

Body Scan for Awareness:

A body scan can uncover the emotional masks we wear and encourage awareness of bodily feelings. Close your eyes and find a comfortable posture to lie down. Beginning with the feelings in your toes, progressively shift your focus to each area of your body until you reach the top of your head. Be mindful of any stress, ache, or unease without passing judgment. This technique can draw attention to the physical manifestations of stress and emotional defenses, motivating us to deal with and overcome these obstacles. It teaches us to pay attention to our bodies and recognize the close connection between our mental and physical moods, which leads to a holistic state of well-being.

Journaling for Self-Discovery:

Spend a few minutes journaling after your meditation. Write down any thoughts, feelings, or sensations that surfaced during your practice. Let your words flow freely; don't censor yourself. This can be an effective tool for revealing concealed pieces of who you are and helping you recognize the masks you wear. You'll start to see themes and patterns that eventually lead back to your true self. Writing in a journal serves as a mirror, reflecting our inner selves and enabling us to see ourselves more clearly. This encourages an honest and self-discovery journey.

Loving-Kindness Meditation for Compassion:

Loving-kindness meditation cultivates empathy for yourself and others, which is essential for peeling away judgmental masks. Pay attention to your breathing at first. Next, say positive affirmations to yourself aloud, like "May I be happy, may I be healthy, may I live with ease." Gradually send these best wishes to family, friends, and even people you disagree with. This exercise awakens the intellect to a more sincere manner of relating to the outside world and softens the heart. It serves as a reminder that having compassion for others and ourselves is essential to living truly and tearing down the barriers preventing us from forming meaningful connections.

Nature Walks for Connection:

Spending time in nature, such as movement meditation, can improve honesty and awareness. Go on a walk outside, preferably in a natural environment, and engage all of your senses. Take note of the scents, sounds, and colors. Feel your feet on the earth. The simplicity and beauty of nature can encourage a closer relationship with the outside world and your actual self. Our relationship with nature grounds us, constantly reminds us of our role in the greater scheme of things, and fosters a sense of authenticity and belonging.

Mindful Listening for Empathy:

When interacting with others, engage in mindful listening. Pay close attention to the speaker; don't prepare your answer in advance. Take note of their tone, body language, and expressions. By dismantling the walls we erect in our relationships, mindful listening can promote more genuine communication and stronger connections. It teaches us the importance of being fully present with another person, a sign of love and respect that makes relationships more sincere and meaningful.

Gratitude Reflections for Perspective:

Consider three things you are grateful for at the end of each day. This can help you resist the push from society to constantly seek more by changing your attention from what you lack to what is abundant in your life. Understanding the importance of the now can help to remove the layers of unhappiness and longing, revealing a more genuine and contented version of oneself. Gratitude helps us see how full our lives are right now and inspires us to accept things with genuine appreciation and an open heart. As Melody Beattie eloquently puts it, *"Gratitude makes sense of our past, brings peace for today, and creates a vision for tomorrow."*

Consistency is Key:

Being authentic through mindfulness and meditation is a process rather than a goal. Practice regularly, even for a short while each day. Over time, these exercises can transform your relationship with yourself and the world, leading to a life with greater purpose, clarity, and joy. The commitment to these practices is a commitment to yourself, a vow to honor your true essence and to navigate life with authenticity and integrity.

In embracing these practices, we embark on a path toward uncovering our genuine selves. Meditation and mindfulness are not just exercises in self-reflection but acts of courage, allowing us to remove the masks we wear and engage with the world with our true essence. Engaging in these practices promotes an authentic existence enhanced by meaningful connections and a keen sense of self. They lead us back to our essence, serving as a light of truth in a society that frequently prioritizes appearance over sincerity.

Trailblazers of Authenticity

In a world often ruled by rigid standards and what's expected, stories of individuals brave enough to live truly serve as potent symbols of courage, resilience, and the indomitable human soul. To be yourself in a world constantly trying to make you something else is the greatest accomplishment," Ralph Waldo Emerson once remarked a sentiment that deeply resonates with the journeys of Marie Curie, Frida Kahlo, Alan Turing, George Takei, and Ella Fitzgerald. These exceptional figures not only shattered the societal forms of their era but also illuminated paths for others to pursue, championing the cause of authenticity in a conforming world. Their journeys, characterized by triumphs over adversity, prejudice, and personal challenges, highlight the transformative might of embracing one's truth and the profound impact such authenticity can have on the world.

Marie Curie: Radiance in the Realm of Science

Marie Curie challenged the gender biases of her era to stand out as a beacon in the realm of science, a field where female presence was minimal. Her journey from Warsaw to Paris, fueled by a relentless desire for learning, led her to surmount not only monetary challenges but also a societal framework that belittled women's scientific contributions. Curie's identification of polonium and radium, along with her trailblazing efforts in radioactivity, secured her Nobel Prizes in Physics and Chemistry, distinguishing her as the first female recipient of such accolades. Her persistence and commitment to scientific exploration shifted conventional perspectives and laid the groundwork for succeeding generations of women in STEM, highlighting the extraordinary possibilities of passionately following one's interests.

Frida Kahlo: The Essence of Unapologetic Self-Expression

Mexican painter Frida Kahlo transformed her distress into a canvas of intense, visually striking artworks that exceeded her era's artistic norms. Afflicted by physical suffering from an early age and later a devastating accident, her resolve remained unbroken. Her self-portraits, rich with symbols from Mexican culture, explored themes of identity, gender, and post-colonialism, challenging societal expectations about femininity and beauty. Kahlo's intertwined art and life were a bold declaration of her unique identity and struggles, symbolizing strength and authenticity for artists and feminists alike.

Alan Turing: Breaking Codes and Stereotypes

Alan Turing, a visionary in mathematics and computer science, was instrumental in decoding the Enigma cipher during World War II, significantly aiding the Allied forces. Despite his substantial contributions, Turing was legally pursued in post-war Britain for his sexual orientation at a period when such matters were criminally charged. Choosing to remain true to his identity in a profoundly intolerant society, Turing's legacy extends beyond his scientific genius; he symbolizes fighting against an oppressive social mold that seeks to define and limit individual identity and love. Turing's posthumous pardon in 2013 highlights the enduring impact of his life, underscoring the importance of living truthfully even when facing unjust laws and social condemnation.

George Takei: Navigating Identity and Activism

George Takei, best known for his role as Hikaru Sulu in the original "Star Trek" series, has navigated his identity as a Japanese American and openly gay man with grace and advocacy that transcends his acting career. Born in Los Angeles, Takei and his family were interned during World War II as part of the U.S. government's incarceration of Japanese Americans. This experience profoundly impacted Takei and fueled his commitment to civil rights activism, particularly for the Asian American and LGBTQ+ communities. Emerging from the shadows later in life, Takei has maximized his platform to champion equality, marriage rights, and social justice, leveraging his celebrity to confront prejudice and spread understanding. His journey underscores how resolving and representing the struggle for acceptance can facilitate progress.

Ella Fitzgerald: Harmonizing Talent and Triumph Over Prejudice

Ella Fitzgerald, known as the "First Lady of Song," broke racial and gender barriers to become one of the most celebrated jazz vocalists in the world. Born in 1917 in Virginia, Fitzgerald encountered a turbulent youth and homelessness before her stunning vocals secured her a spot on the Apollo Theater's Amateur Night stage. Despite the pervasive racial discrimination of the era, Fitzgerald's talents propelled her to fame, collaborating with legends including Duke Ellington and Louis Armstrong. She used her artistry to navigate and challenge the societal constraints of her time, becoming the first African American woman to win a Grammy Award. Her success is evidence of the transformative power of resilience and the universal language of music in breaking down societal barriers. These stories illuminate the diversity of paths toward living with authenticity and purpose. By embracing their truth and challenging the norms of their times, each individual contributed uniquely to the ever-evolving fabric of human progress. Their lives remind us that authenticity demands courage and can significantly impact society, inspiring future generations to live openly and truthfully.

Chapter 2: From Self-Doubt to Self-Belief - A Spiritual Awakening

"Faith is taking the first step even when you don't see the whole staircase."

-Martin Luther King Jr.

Self-doubt is an emotional challenge that affects many individuals, acting as a significant barrier to realizing one's spiritual potential. Understanding where self-doubt comes from and recognizing how it impacts personal growth can provide insights into overcoming this obstacle to tap into deeper spiritual realms. Indeed, realizing that such doubts often emerge from our past can empower us to face them with more courage and faith.

Self-doubt frequently results from a combination of external and internal factors. It may originate internally from a person's critical self-talk, which frequently centers on missed opportunities or rejections. Such thoughts can make individuals believe that these negative experiences define their capabilities, reinforcing feelings of inadequacy. External cultural norms and societal expectations significantly impact how people see themselves. Self-doubt can develop when people discover they are not living up to these social norms, leading them to second-guess their decisions and life's course. However, faith encourages looking beyond these limitations, urging us to step forward even without clear direction.

Family background and early life events also play a role in the development of self-doubt. Parenting approaches that are excessively protective or critical, for example, can prevent kids from taking on obstacles and growing from their failures—

experiences that are vital for boosting self-esteem. On the other hand, self-doubt can be avoided in a supportive setting that encourages attempting new things and accepts failure as a necessary part of learning. A resilient faith can be established through such nurture, enabling people to face life's uncertainties with greater assurance.

When thinking about the spiritual path, self-doubt is a major barrier. Spirituality often demands a strong sense of self and reliance on one's intuition. Self-doubt undermines this reliance, clouding judgment and weakening the connection to one's spiritual instincts. This can make it difficult to pursue a true spiritual path and fully embrace personal spiritual beliefs. To overcome these barriers, we must cultivate a faith that does not require seeing the entire staircase, allowing us to take the first step in trust.

Furthermore, the path to spiritual growth usually involves going through periods of uncertainty and deep existential questions. These are natural but can become overwhelming if intensified by persistent self-doubt. When individuals doubt their spiritual experiences or beliefs, they might be more inclined to dismiss these pivotal moments rather than explore them, missing out on potential insights and deeper understanding. Therefore, embracing faith in the face of uncertainty can transform self-doubt into a tool for deeper spiritual exploration.

Understanding the pervasive nature of self-doubt can indeed reveal its subtler impacts on both daily life and long-term aspirations. This emotional barrier often infiltrates our lives in ways that are not immediately obvious, subtly shaping our decisions and behaviors over time. By fostering faith in oneself, one can more effectively confront and traverse the doubts that arise, potentially leading to significant personal and spiritual growth.

Self-doubt does not solely arise during moments of significant life choices or profound spiritual questioning; it frequently manifests in the quieter, more mundane moments of life. These small instances of doubt, though seemingly insignificant on their own, can accumulate and have a profound cumulative effect. Each moment of doubt can act like a small anchor, holding individuals back from taking steps that might lead to personal growth or happiness. Faith, then, becomes a critical force, propelling us forward despite the shadows of doubt.

For example, in daily interactions or decisions, self-doubt might prevent someone from expressing their true thoughts or from taking initiative in a group setting. Over time, failing to act or speak out can lead to missed opportunities for learning, relationship building, or professional advancement. In a spiritual context, these small doubts can deter individuals from exploring new practices, attending community events, or simply sharing their experiences with others, which are all activities that can enrich one's spiritual journey. Through faith, one can begin to overcome these small doubts, embracing each opportunity as a step toward greater spiritual fulfillment.

Moreover, self-doubt can affect a person's openness to seizing new opportunities. Feelings of inadequacy or concern about potentially failing can hinder applying for a job, taking up a new pastime, or even reaching out to meet new friends. Though they may all appear insignificant, these activities are vital stages that can lead to a more fulfilling life. By adopting a faith-driven approach, people can see past their uncertainties and anxieties by taking each step with hope and trust instead of complete certainty.

On a broader scale, the accumulative effect of daily self-doubt can shape an individual's life trajectory. It can lead to a life path more about avoiding failure than pursuing passion or fulfillment. This avoidance can manifest as staying in unsatisfying but secure job positions, remaining in unfulfilling relationships, or preceding any form of personal risk that might lead to a more rewarding existence. By shifting the focus from fear to faith, one can redefine one's journey, choosing paths that may be less certain but potentially more enriching and aligned with one's true passions and spiritual aspirations.

In spirituality, consider the situation where an individual regularly engages in meditation and spiritual gatherings, seeking deeper understanding and connection. However, despite occasional profound moments of peace and insight during these practices, this person begins questioning the authenticity of these experiences. Doubts arise about whether these moments are genuine spiritual connections or merely figments of the imagination. This skepticism is rooted in a deep-seated uncertainty about their own spiritual adequacy and the validity of their experiences. Adopting a perspective of faith can alleviate these doubts, encouraging a more open and trusting engagement with spiritual practices.

This self-doubt also spills over into their participation within their spiritual community. The person hesitates when given the chance to lead conversations or offer insights because they are afraid they don't know enough or would mislead others. They are unable to participate fully because of these worries, which hinders their personal development and ability to give back to the community. People can become more involved and powerful in their spiritual communities and foster growth in others by developing a faith that endures in the midst of uncertainty.

Over time, this cycle of doubt and hesitation can lead to a spiritual life that feels stagnant and unfulfilling. Instead of progressing on their spiritual path, the individual remains stuck, unable to fully embrace and explore the depth of their spiritual experiences. The faith and enthusiasm that formerly drove their spiritual endeavors may eventually be undermined by this stagnation, which can also cause them to feel disconnected from their group and from their own spiritual journey. Thus, acknowledging and dealing with the ubiquitous nature of self-doubt improves a person's quality of life on a daily basis and deepens their spiritual development. By acknowledging and confronting the small, everyday manifestations of self-doubt, people can progressively cultivate a more self-assured, proactive, and spiritually fulfilling life. They can go through and beyond doubt and toward a more satisfying and spiritually rich life if they use their faith as a compass.

Spiritual Practices that Build Self-Worth and Confidence

Building on the above foundation, exploring specific spiritual practices that directly contribute to strengthening self-worth and confidence is vital. Spiritual practices are crucial in strengthening one's self-worth and confidence in the journey toward personal growth and development. Through participation in endeavors that enhance one's connection to the self and the wider cosmos, people can develop a more robust sense of self and empowerment. This inner fortitude provides a strong basis for handling life's different obstacles and gives the person a steadfast sense of capability and resilience. As the Dalai Lama wisely said, *"The roots of all goodness lie in the soil of appreciation for goodness."* This underlines the transformative power of spiritual practices in cultivating an appreciation for one's inner strength and virtues.

Yoga

Yoga is a spiritual activity that greatly cultivates self-esteem and assurance through physical postures, controlled breathing, and meditation. Yoga aids in synchronizing the body, mind, and spirit. This synergy guarantees that participants focus on their physical health and boost their mental clarity and emotional stability.

The physical component of yoga especially increases bodily consciousness and wellness, inevitably enhancing one's view of oneself. People have a more positive attitude about themselves when they become more aware of their bodies' demands and capabilities.

Regular yoga practice requires discipline, which helps people realize they can commit to and achieve personal goals. This builds a strong feeling of self-esteem in people. Building a robust self-concept is greatly aided by this consistent dedication to personal development and self-care. Beyond only enhancing physical health, yoga's comprehensive approach makes its practitioners feel more centered and self-assured, prepared to confront life with a revitalized spirit and vitality. People learn a potent instrument for self-transformation through yoga, which gives them the peace of mind and newfound energy to face life's obstacles.

Affirmations and Positive Visualization

Affirmations involve the practice of positive thinking and self-empowerment—fostering a belief that a positive mental attitude supported by affirmations will achieve success in anything. This practice helps to overwrite negative, limiting beliefs that individuals may hold about themselves with positive, empowering thoughts, which can gradually improve their self-esteem and self-worth. Affirmations strengthen mental resilience, which is crucial for maintaining a healthy self-image and achieving personal goals.

Positive visualization, on the other hand, entails imagining a desired result to assist in realizing the imagined situation. Visualizing success in great detail in one's mind can cultivate a greater sense of confidence in one's capacity to accomplish one's goals. This practice encourages action toward reaching personal goals while also boosting self-confidence. By visualizing the processes required to achieve a goal, positive visualization acts as a mental rehearsal, readying the mind and body for success.

Participation in Spiritual Community Activities

Engaging with a spiritual community can significantly enhance an individual's sense of belonging and self-worth. Participation in a spiritual community markedly improves a person's feeling of inclusion and self-value. Joining a group that upholds similar values and beliefs offers a supportive framework that promotes personal development. Within these groups, members are enveloped by supportive peers who offer motivation and comprehension, enhancing a robust sense of unity and shared intent. Involvement in group activities can further elevate one's purpose and identity, thereby increasing assurance and self-value.

This sense of community support provides a safe foundation from which people can confidently explore their spirituality and personal development. When community members observe and encourage one another on their journeys, the experience of growth and exploration as a group can be immensely inspiring and validating. People who participate in this way frequently discover that they can provide and receive assistance, which enhances their sense of value and contribution and reinforces their place in the group.

Service to Others

Serving others is also a spiritual practice that improves one's sense of worth by causing one to put others before oneself. Being altruistic can help lessen emotions of inadequacy and self-doubt since helping others makes one feel important and helpful.

People who volunteer frequently report feeling less overwhelmed by their personal issues and gaining a more positive outlook on life. Giving to others can help foster a sense of community by emphasizing the common experiences of all people and lowering feelings of loneliness. Serving others can also help put one's own problems into perspective and frequently show that all share personal issues. This broadened perspective significantly enhances one's feeling of connection and self-assurance and improves one's ability to make a positive impact. Participating in service activities enables individuals to move beyond their personal experiences and observe the shared aspects of human challenges and achievements, nurturing a deeper understanding of the unity of all lives. This awareness can strengthen one's confidence and lessen the influence of self-doubt, as they directly witness the constructive shifts their efforts can provoke in others.

Nature Connection

Connecting with nature is a spiritual activity that promotes inner tranquility and introspection. Time spent in natural environments can soothe the mind and decrease stress, leading to a more transparent evaluation of one's life and self. The simplicity and allure of nature encourage individuals to slow down and relish the moment, promoting awareness and a greater appreciation for the small joys of life. This bond also aids individuals in recognizing and valuing the simple beauties within themselves, enhancing a sense of value and connection to the world.

Nature is a potent symbol of the natural processes of growth and rejuvenation, mirroring our spiritual and personal development paths. Observing how nature adapts, endures, and thrives can act as an analogy for human experiences, providing valuable insights into resilience and renewal. This natural reflection can inspire individuals to accept their growth paths, valuing both the highs and lows as vital elements of their personal evolution and spiritual path.

Chanting and Mantras

Chanting and using mantras are deep spiritual practices that can increase confidence and self-worth. This technique, which entails repeating holy words or phrases, is said to focus spiritual energy and cleanse the mind. Chanting is said to have a calming effect on the body and spirit because of its rhythmic and repetitive nature, which also helps to reduce stress and anxiety. Mantras are often statements of perseverance, strength, and serenity that can transform a person's inner dialogue and promote a more positive self-image.

Participating in group chanting can strengthen these benefits by creating a bond between participants and a common spiritual experience. This group practice offers a potent blend of individual reflection and group support by fortifying spiritual resonance on a personal level and improving feelings of connectedness with others. People can cultivate a more centered and grounded approach to their spiritual journey by regularly engaging in chanting and mantras. This will help them overcome self-doubt and embrace their path with clarity and confidence.

Incorporating spiritual activities into everyday life can result in significant gains in confidence and self-worth. Every activity, whether chanting, mantras, yoga, meditation, or community involvement, has special advantages that can aid people in realizing their worth and potential. As these activities get deeper, they contribute to a more meaningful and fulfilling life and enhance personal growth. These practices are more than just rituals; they are means of realizing and reaffirming one's potential and value in a constantly changing world.

Power of Faith: Stories of Transformation

Faith and belief often form the foundation upon which individuals build the strength to overcome significant challenges. Throughout history, countless individuals have underlined the transformative power of faith, showing how deeply held beliefs can lead to dramatic changes in one's circumstances and outlook.

Nelson Mandela: A Legacy of Faith and Reconciliation

Nelson Mandela's journey provides a profound example of how steadfast belief and faith can lead to monumental changes in an individual's life and across the nation. Mandela's unwavering faith in justice and equality guided him through 27 years of imprisonment. His commitment to understanding and peacemaking over retaliation helped to ensure a smooth transition to democracy after his release. Mandela's story demonstrates how people can inspire millions of people around the world to influence change by combining firm patience and tenacity with confidence in a just cause.

Victor Frankl: Finding Meaning through Adversity

Another moving account of how faith may turn personal despair into a chance for great understanding and enlightenment is provided by the Austrian neurologist and psychiatrist Victor Frankl, a Holocaust survivor. Frankl came up with the idea that people may find meaning in their suffering by choosing how they would internally react to it, even in the most horrific and degrading situations, while he was living in Nazi concentration camps. His well-known quote, "When we are no longer able to change a situation, we are challenged to change ourselves," perfectly captures this idea. Because of his belief that people can choose their attitude in any situation, Viktor Frankl established logotherapy, a type of psychotherapy that holds that people's main motivation is not pleasure but rather the search for meaning in life.

Karoly Takacs: Triumph over Adversity

The story of Karoly Takacs, a sergeant in the Hungarian Army, provides another vivid example of faith's power. Takacs was a world-class shooter, but a grenade explosion severely injured his right hand, which was also his shooting hand, during military training in 1938. Despite this career-ending injury, he secretly taught himself to shoot with his left hand. His faith in his abilities and determination saw him return to shooting and win two Olympic gold medals in 1948 and 1952, competing in events requiring hand use. Takacs did not see his disability as an impediment but a challenge to overcome, driven by profound belief in his capabilities and potential.

John Newton: From Slave Trader to Abolitionist

Faith can have a transformational effect on one's healing and rehabilitation, in addition to helping one overcome obstacles in the political or physical spheres.

This is best shown by the life of John Newton, a former slave trader who became a clergyman and abolitionist. Following a profound spiritual conversion, Newton gave up his previous life and became an opponent of the slave trade. His newly discovered faith profoundly changed his actions and perspective, leading him from a man who caused great pain to one who fought for its abolition. His hymn "Amazing Grace," which captures his own conversion and redemption through faith, is a testament to this change.

While differing in terms of setting and people, these stories are united by the idea that faith may have a profound impact on individual and societal transformation. Whether through the resilience shown by Mandela, the philosophical insights of Frankl, the determination of Takacs, or the repentance and reform of Newton, each narrative demonstrates that faith, coupled with action, can lead us through seemingly insurmountable obstacles to a place of profound personal and collective achievement.

As the proverb goes, *"Faith can move mountains,"* showing that even the most daunting challenges can be overcome with deep belief. Through these examples, it becomes evident that faith is not just a personal comfort but a powerful catalyst for change.

Key Exercises for Strengthening Belief and Enhancing Spiritual Connection

Belief and spiritual connection form the base of many people's lives, providing a sense of purpose, direction, and resilience. Strengthening these aspects of the self can lead to improved mental health, greater happiness, and a deeper sense of fulfillment.

Focusing on these areas can also enhance one's ability to cope with stress and adversity, grounding individuals in a stable sense of self and purpose. This enhanced grounding helps foster a clear and calm mind, essential for making thoughtful decisions and facing life's challenges with a stronger disposition. Enhancing spiritual connections can also improve emotional intelligence and promote a better understanding of oneself and others.

1. Scripture Reading and Interpretative Discussion

Reading and interpreting spiritual texts can be immensely enriching for those who follow a religious path. This exercise involves reading passages slowly and thoughtfully, then contemplating or discussing their meanings and how they apply to one's life. Engaging with texts can deepen understanding and make one's spiritual practices more meaningful. It can also encourage a lifelong habit of learning and spiritual curiosity. Moreover, these discussions can lead to new insights and deeper revelations that can be transformative, enhancing one's spiritual journey and personal growth. Delving into these discussions often prompts a profound re-evaluation of personal beliefs and a strengthened commitment to spiritual principles.

Reading and analyzing spiritual books can be enlightening for religious people. This reading activity entails reading texts slowly and carefully, then reflecting on or talking about their meanings and applications to one's own life. This kind of interaction with books can enhance comprehension and add significance to one's spiritual activities. Additionally, it can foster a lifetime curiosity about spirituality and learning. Furthermore, these conversations may result in profound revelations and fresh perspectives that have the power to change lives and advance spiritual development. Engaging in these conversations frequently leads to a deep reassessment of one's own beliefs and a heightened dedication to spiritual values.

2. Cultivating Gratitude

Cultivating gratitude is an exercise that involves taking time each day to reflect on the things one is thankful for. This can be done through writing a list of gratitude items, sharing these thoughts with a friend or family member, or meditating on feelings of thankfulness. Practicing gratitude regularly can lead to changes in the way one views the world, fostering a positive mindset and a deeper appreciation for life's blessings, which are core aspects of many spiritual paths. Through constant awareness of life's gifts, this practice improves emotional well-being and fortifies spiritual ties. Furthermore, consistent appreciation practice can profoundly change an individual's emotional reactions, increasing empathy, decreasing aggression, and strengthening interpersonal bonds. This shift can profoundly alter how people interact with the outside world, improving their and others' lives.

3. Mindful Walking

Mindful walking encourages an active awareness that unites body and mind by combining the physical exercise of walking with mindfulness. Walking can assist in synchronizing the mind and body in a meditative state; this can be practiced in a park, quiet neighborhood, or even outside. This activity may be incredibly relaxing and spiritually enlightening as it promotes a heightened sense of awareness and presence, enhances circulation, and relieves tension. Moreover, mindful walking offers a unique opportunity to develop a dynamic, environment-adaptable meditation practice that raises spiritual awareness in everyday settings.

4. Engaging with Sacred Music

Sacred music can be performed or listened to raise the soul and strengthen one's spiritual ties. Through the ability to transcend mental limitations and communicate directly with the soul, music can elicit strong emotional and spiritual reactions that are both uplifting and restorative. Engaging with music this way can lead to unexpected emotional revelations and a deeper spiritual unity. This spiritual practice can be a strong form of meditation and reflection, allowing listeners or performers to experience a transcendent connection to their inner self and the divine.

5. Spiritual Retreats

People can escape the daily grind and immerse themselves in spiritual activities with like-minded people by taking part in spiritual retreats. Retreats often offer a combination of meditation, teachings, community living, and personal reflection time, which can intensify one's spiritual experience and provide renewed motivation for spiritual practices.

These retreats are helpful for restoring one's spiritual energy to a high degree and can support ongoing spiritual practices by offering new insights and a rekindled sense of passion. The immersion experience strengthens the dedication to one's own spiritual development by enabling a closer relationship with spiritual teachings and the community.

6. Acts of Service and Charity

Direct action, such as serving others and giving to charities, can strengthen spiritual values and beliefs. In addition to helping others, these deeds also deepen the giver's spiritual life by highlighting how interconnected all people are and encouraging a sense of empathy and community.

Regularly performing charity deeds can significantly change a person's perspective from self-centered behavior to a more community-focused style of living, which is crucial for both personal and spiritual development. This practice is a keystone of spiritual development since it transforms and improves personal empathy and practical application of spiritual ideals.

By integrating these exercises into daily life, individuals can cultivate a richer, more meaningful spiritual experience and reinforce their foundational beliefs, leading to a more purposeful and centered life. These practices help build resilience, enhance personal well-being, and deepen connections with others and the world, forming a comprehensive approach to spiritual development.

Chapter 3: Imperfections as Strengths - The Beauty of Being Broken

"Embrace your imperfections; they make you who you are."

This reminder sets the stage for understanding that accepting our flaws is a fundamental step toward deeper spiritual connection and improved psychological well-being. This journey involves recognizing our imperfections as obstacles and opportunities for growth and self-discovery. It begins with an understanding of what constitutes a flaw. Traits such as impatience, stubbornness, or a propensity to worry are common aspects of our character or behavior that we often view negatively. While these might initially seem detrimental, they are intrinsically human and universal.

Acknowledging them not only promotes personal acceptance but also invites us to explore deeper insights into our behavior and emotions, recognizing these traits as signals of underlying needs or unresolved conflicts. This acknowledgment is the first crucial step toward growth, as it shifts our perspective from criticism to curiosity, opening the door to self-compassion and empathy.

By accepting our flaws, we may actively interact with them and investigate how and why they arise in our day-to-day experiences. Insights about our psychological tendencies and emotional needs can be gained from this investigation, which can result in more useful personal development techniques. An underlying urge for efficiency or control, for example, can be the cause of impatience. By realizing this, we may deal with our behavior's underlying causes as opposed to just its symptoms. In a similar vein, admitting our stubbornness might help us identify our fear of vulnerability or change, which will motivate us to work on opening up and becoming more adaptable. This deeper engagement is beneficial to our spiritual lives as well as our self-knowledge since many spiritual traditions teach that true learning comes from accepting our entire selves—flaws and all—into our lives. This all-encompassing method promotes a profound sense of peace and unity with the wider human experience, cultivating a more understanding and accepting mindset toward both oneself and other people.

Self-acceptance is pivotal in embracing these parts of ourselves. It entails accepting, without passing judgment, every facet of who we are, flaws and all. Self-compassion is nurtured here, and mental health depends on it. We can considerably lessen the internal conflict resulting from self-criticism and denial by accepting who we are. As Carl Jung once said, *"I am not what happened to me. I am what I choose to become."* This viewpoint is essential for moving toward self-acceptance and development. Adopting this perspective enables us to take proactive measures for our own progress, turning perceived shortcomings into opportunities for development and improvement. This improves our capacity to deal with life's obstacles.

From a psychological standpoint, accepting our imperfections helps us feel less stressed and anxious about trying to achieve perfection, which is an impossible goal that can make us feel inadequate and like failures. Accepting our flaws releases pressure that can cause major mental health problems like anxiety and depression by enabling us to have more reasonable expectations for ourselves. In addition to accepting who we are, this stage involves allowing ourselves to be open to the potential of real self-improvement that comes from a place of love rather than judgment. For instance, someone who is aware of their propensity for procrastination may begin to comprehend the fear of failure that motivates it. They can approach activities more compassionate and inspiringly by addressing this fear, lowering anxiety, and increasing productivity.

This acceptance has the power to change how we respond to obstacles and failures. We can accept mistakes as inevitable components of the learning process rather than seeing them as personal failings. This change in viewpoint can greatly lessen the fear of attempting new things and promote a development mentality in which obstacles are viewed as chances to improve rather than as dangers to our self-worth. This more positive outlook reduces stress and anxiety while improving psychological flexibility, making it easier for us to adjust to changes and recover from setbacks. Such psychological resilience is essential for long-term well-being and continuous personal growth.

In a spiritual sense, embracing our imperfections unites us with other world's spiritual traditions that prioritize humility and acknowledging our limitations as human beings.

Recognizing and embracing our shortcomings can be perceived as a humble gesture, bringing us into line with the fact that we are a member of the more flawed human race. Because we are no longer at odds with our own nature, this knowledge leads to a feeling of happiness and serenity and opens the door to forgiveness of both others and ourselves. Building more harmonious interpersonal and social connections requires this kind of forgiveness. Moreover, this spiritual alignment inspires us to accept the idea of shared humanity, in which realizing our limits results in a stronger bond with the universe or the divine. Our spiritual activities can benefit from this relationship by becoming more meaningful and practically based.

For instance, mindfulness practice in Buddhism teaches us to observe our thoughts and feelings objectively, which enables us to accept our flaws. This acceptance is viewed as a means of developing compassion for both ourselves and other people, not as a sign of giving up. Spiritual traditions impart through these activities that accepting our imperfections can result in increased insight and a deeper spiritual connection.

Adding to this spiritual journey, the act of accepting our flaws also facilitates a profound transformation within our inner selves. It prompts us to release the misconception of total control and perfection, which often restricts us to unattainable ideals and persistent dissatisfaction. As a spiritual guide, Leonard Cohen expressed, *"There is a crack in everything. That's how the light gets in."* This statement beautifully shows that our shortcomings are not just faults but gateways to development and enlightenment.

Through these cracks, we make room for development and the entrance of new understandings and illumination, deepening our spiritual experiences and understanding of the universe. This transformation is gradual, not immediate, a steady realization that enhances our spiritual maturity and helps us find comfort in the beauty of our imperfections. By accepting our own flaws, we develop greater empathy and understanding toward others, recognizing that we are all similarly flawed. This recognition can help us connect with others more authentically, which in turn deepens our relationships and enhances our sense of community and belonging. This compassion widens the impact of our self-acceptance to the larger societal context, nurturing a kinder and more empathetic world.

By demonstrating self-acceptance, we motivate others to face and embrace their shortcomings, initiating a chain reaction that can reshape communities. This cycle of acceptance and empathy not only fortifies personal connections but also cultivates a more welcoming and supportive communal atmosphere, which is crucial for collective health.

Embracing Imperfections

In the journey of personal development, embracing our imperfections plays a critical role in fostering resilience and promoting significant growth. Below are several real-life examples and personal stories that show how accepting personal flaws can catalyze transformative experiences and lead to a more fulfilled life.

From Setback to Comeback

John's peers had always considered him to be a perfectionist. He aimed for perfection in every line of code during his time working as a software engineer. But this constant quest for excellence frequently left him stressed out and never completely content with his achievements. The pivotal moment occurred during a project that took longer than anticipated. John faced criticism and, for the first time, faced his fear of failing. John felt a new feeling of freedom when he accepted that he was imperfect and that he could learn from his mistakes. This change in viewpoint enabled him to tackle his task with greater creativity and less anxiety, resulting in inventions he had previously dismissed as unthinkable. The story of John shows how accepting our shortcomings can shift a debilitating fear of failure into a driving force for creativity and personal achievement. As the saying goes, *"A diamond with a flaw is worth more than a pebble without imperfections."*

Healing through Vulnerability

Lisa, a seasoned public speaker, always felt she had to maintain an image of strength and composure. However, she struggled with anxiety, which would often intensify just before her speeches. It wasn't until she chose to share her struggles with her audience during a particularly large conference that she truly connected with them.

This act of vulnerability turned into her strength, deeply resonating with many who admired her courage to be authentic. Her career was further boosted by the experience, as organizations started to seek her out for her sincere approach to challenging subjects, in addition to improving her mental health. Lisa's story shows how embracing and sharing our vulnerabilities may increase our resilience and create stronger bonds with others.

Transforming Flaws into Stepping Stones

Michael, a young entrepreneur, frequently faced criticism for his impulsive decision-making. Initially defensive, he began to see a pattern where some of his impulsive decisions led to unexpected successes while others resulted in learning opportunities. By recognizing this trait as a double-edged sword, he sought to understand the underlying drives of his behavior, channeling his impulsivity into calculated risks. Using this approach not only helped him launch additional profitable businesses but also enabled him to teach other aspiring business owners the value of striking a balance between risk and reflection.

The story of Michael exemplifies how what we may view as a drawback can actually be utilized to fuel personal and professional advancement. As Warren Buffett aptly stated, *"Risk comes from not knowing what you're doing."* Michael's experience highlights the value of embracing and refining our natural tendencies to realize their full potential.

Cultivating Growth from Self-Reflection

Angela, a writer known for her critical self-assessment, often found herself bogged down by self-doubt. Her breakthrough came when she began to use her critical nature constructively by applying it to refine her writing process instead of allowing it to undermine her confidence. This subtle shift helped her produce a bestselling novel that was celebrated for its depth and insight. Angela's ability to transform her critical self-view into a tool for improvement highlights how recognizing and adjusting our response to our imperfections can lead to profound achievements. This transition not only solidified her reputation in the literary world but also inspired her to conduct workshops, teaching other writers how to harness their self-critique constructively for artistic success.

Building Resilience through Creative Rebound

David, an architect, faced severe setbacks early in his career when his innovative designs were repeatedly rejected for being too avant-garde. Each rejection felt like a critique of his core vision. Instead of conforming to traditional designs to secure more immediate approvals, David embraced his unique creative vision as an essential part of his identity. He started working with innovators who shared his values, and finally, he was successful in specialized markets that appreciated modern design and sustainability. David's story demonstrates how, despite initial setbacks, staying true to one's artistic principles may help one discover one's proper place in the field and eventually open doors to greater recognition and prosperity.

Embracing Imperfection in Leadership

Emma, a corporate leader, was known for her decisive nature but criticized for her lack of flexibility. This trait, often seen as a flaw, initially isolated her from her team. However, Emma decided to address this by openly discussing her leadership style with her team and soliciting their feedback. This openness to learning and adaptability transformed her relationship with her team, fostering a more collaborative and supportive environment.

It also allowed her to develop a more adaptive leadership style that valued contributions from others, enhancing team effectiveness and morale. Emma's story is a testament to how leaders can turn perceived flaws into opportunities for personal growth and team development. As Ralph Waldo Emerson once said, *"Our strength grows out of our weaknesses."* Emma's path is highlighted in this quote, which demonstrates how our weakest points may also serve as our greatest assets. These stories underline a broader principle: Our imperfections are not just hurdles but integral elements of our personal narratives that lead to resilience, development, and a profound comprehension of our abilities.

By embracing our flaws, we open ourselves to a realm of possibilities where resilience stems from self-acceptance and courage and where advancement is ongoing. These stories act as both motivation and a guide for leading a more authentic and satisfying life.

Considering these stories, we might ponder, "How can recognizing and embracing my own flaws contribute to greater personal development and resilience in my life?" This question challenges us to think about how our imperfections might change us and to embrace them as chances for growth and self-awareness.

Wabi-Sabi Wisdom: Celebrating Imperfection in Ourselves and the World Around Us

"Nothing lasts, nothing is finished, and nothing is perfect." This perspective captures the essence of wabi-sabi, a Japanese philosophy that emphasizes the beauty of imperfection in the natural decay and aging of objects. It is an aesthetic sensibility that finds depth and significance in the flawed, the decayed, and the incomplete.

This philosophy extends beyond mere acceptance of imperfection; it is about embracing it as an essential component of beauty and authenticity. It nurtures an acceptance that everything is temporary and encourages us to appreciate the fleeting moments of beauty in our daily lives. The rustic, the weathered, and the worn are celebrated, reflecting a profound appreciation for the natural cycle of growth and decay.

Wabi-sabi first emerged in the ancient Japanese tea ceremony. Here, plain and rustic surroundings and equipment consciously mirror the wabi-sabi principles of modesty and simplicity. The philosophy emphasizes that beauty is ephemeral and subjective and invites a deeper awareness of life's fleeting nature. It rejects the contemporary fixation on perfection and fosters an appreciation for what is modest, unrefined, and natural.

This cultural ethos extends into various aspects of Japanese life, including art, architecture, and landscaping. In these practices, the impermanent, the tattered, or the incomplete are embraced and considered part of the aesthetic appeal. For example, in the art of kintsugi, broken pottery is repaired with gold-laced lacquer to highlight, rather than hide, the damage. This art form celebrates each artifact's unique history by emphasizing its fractures and repairs instead of camouflaging them.

This appreciation of visible repair highlights the beauty of resilience and recovery, teaching that there is elegance in survival and renewal. Additionally, this practice metaphorically underlines the value of embracing our flaws and imperfections, reflecting a profound philosophical acceptance that goes beyond the physical. Wabi-sabi provides a powerful lens through which we can see ourselves and our lives in the context of self-acceptance. It teaches that flaws are not signs of weakness but rather of individuality and originality. This viewpoint can change the way we think about personal development and self-worth, helping us to have a better relationship with ourselves.

We can let go of our critical opinions and adopt a more understanding and welcoming attitude toward our flaws, whether they be psychological or physical scars, by internalizing wabi-sabi. This philosophy not only aids in our self-acceptance but also acts as a reminder that our unique characteristics and perceived flaws are what make us human.

To apply wabi-sabi to self-acceptance, we must first acknowledge our flaws, whether intellectual, emotional, or physical, and embrace that these are what make each of us special.

It pushes us to let go of our unattainable expectations of perfection and self-criticism, which frequently result in self-rejection and unhappiness. This way of thinking encourages us to take pride in the parts of ourselves that are less polished and help us realize their worth. It stands as a reminder that real, unfiltered beauty and strength come from inside, not from the unrealistic standards frequently presented by the media and popular culture. Adopting this way of thinking can free us from the constraints of conformity and let our genuine selves emerge and shine.

For instance, consider someone who struggles with insecurity about their abilities. Wabi-sabi invites this person to view their perceived shortcomings as chances for development and education rather than as inborn failings. Increased resilience and a readiness to take chances and rise to challenges can result from this mentality change. This way of thinking emphasizes the beauty of becoming rather than the stress of aiming for an ideal condition, giving a reassuring reassurance that it's acceptable to be a work in progress. It creates an atmosphere in which every effort and setback is viewed as an essential component of the trip, enhancing our quality of life and advancing our individual development.

Additionally, wabi-sabi can affect how we communicate with other people. We can cultivate more empathy and comprehension for the shortcomings of others by embracing our own inadequacies.

Our relationships may improve as a result, fostering a community that is more welcoming and encouraging. It fosters an empathetic society in which we acknowledge that everyone, including ourselves, is struggling with their flaws and confronting challenges. Stronger, more meaningful connections may be formed, and gaps can be filled with this common knowledge. By looking at things through this lens, we can value sincerity and authenticity over perfection and learn to see the beauty in the flawed connections we create.

Living with a wabi-sabi mindset might entail writing in a notebook about our flaws and reinterpreting them as qualities that enhance and enliven our narratives.

It could also entail making the decision to value setbacks just as highly as achievements, viewing each as a crucial stepping stone toward our own growth. Having this kind of thinking promotes a way of living that values imperfection and views life as a lovely sequence of moments, each with its own flaws and lessons. It increases our sense of well-being and contentment by encouraging us to appreciate the innate flaws in the universe and to find delight in the commonplace. Wabi-sabi also instills in us the need to live simply and authentically. It might encourage someone to simplify their home and only maintain truly useful or meaningful items, making their surroundings a true reflection of who they are.

This way of thinking can permeate our relationships and decisions, encouraging a less materialistic and more sensible way of living. It inspires us to concentrate on the important things in life and discover joy and beauty in the simplicity all around us. Through wabi-sabi, we learn to appreciate what we have and to live more mindfully and purposefully, emphasizing quality over quantity in every aspect of life.

Moreover, this mindset can be incredibly freeing in today's society, where perfection is often pursued—whether in our professional roles, personal relationships, or physical looks. Adopting wabi-sabi allows us to experience fulfillment and pleasure in "existing" rather than constantly striving to improve or change. This mindset fosters a more tranquil life, where we stop pursuing elusive perfection and start appreciating the charm in what already is. Through wabi-sabi, we realize that our flaws are not obstacles to joy but are actually the components that enrich and embellish our existence.

Through this acceptance, we attain a deeper and more compassionate comprehension of ourselves, leading to authentic joy and inner calm. By adopting wabi-sabi in our daily routines, we start to value the perfect in the imperfect, viewing our imperfections as attributes that enrich, rather than detract from, our life stories. This approach teaches us to value the rough, the imperfect, and the fleeting and to discover delight and tranquility in the natural flaws that shape our human experiences. As the Japanese proverb says, *"Even monkeys fall from trees,"* reminding us that everyone makes mistakes and that imperfection is part of being human. This proverb captures the spirit of wabi-sabi, encouraging us to embrace our flaws and the natural course of life with acceptance and humility.

Guided Practices for Celebrating Our Unique Selves

Acknowledging and celebrating our flaws as integral parts of our unique selves is empowering and liberating in our journey toward self-acceptance. This guide offers practical steps to help you embrace your imperfections, foster a healthier relationship with yourself, and enhance your overall well-being.

1. Comparison with Others

Engaging in practices focusing on comparing oneself to others can decrease self-esteem and satisfaction. Instead, it is advantageous to concentrate on one's development and accomplishments without comparing them to those of others. In a way that honors your distinct journey and qualities, this fosters on going personal development and a more positive self-perception. Happiness and a sense of achievement are enhanced when personal accomplishments are honored instead of rivalry and comparisons. Such a practice nurtures a positive mental environment where personal victories are celebrated without the shadow of others' achievements. This approach promotes a constructive inward focus that reduces feelings of inadequacy and increases confidence. It supports the development of a positive mindset that emphasizes personal growth and self-realization by highlighting individual talents and qualities, fostering a more meaningful and self-affirming path through life.

2. Overly Critical Self-Evaluation

Engaging in practices that involve too much self-critique can greatly affect one's psychological well-being and self-perception. It's crucial to conduct self-assessments with an even-handed view, recognizing both strengths and areas needing growth without self-condemnation. This balanced method encourages progress while maintaining self-kindness and respect for one's own journey. Offering oneself helpful feedback can aid in personal growth and increase self-consciousness. Cultivating an environment of self-kindness rather than self-critique enhances motivation and a positive self-perception, both essential for stable mental and emotional health. Additionally, this strategy supports resilience, enabling one to tackle challenges with a reinforced sense of identity and a reduced tendency to absorb failures, contributing to improved mental health.

3. Perfectionism in Practice

Perfectionism can be limiting and damaging when it impedes personal progress or enjoyment in activities. Practices should promote doing one's best without the unrealistic expectation of perfection. This approach helps maintain motivation and satisfaction, fostering a healthy mindset that values effort and personal bests rather than flawless outcomes. Reducing the pressure of perfection can also decrease anxiety and increase creativity in personal and professional endeavors. Embracing imperfection as a natural part of the human experience can liberate one from the chains of unattainable standards, enhancing personal satisfaction and creativity. This mindset shift helps build resilience and flexibility, key qualities for navigating life's inevitable ups and downs and embracing challenges with an open heart.

4. Ignoring Personal Boundaries

Respecting personal boundaries and not pushing oneself or others into uncomfortable or potentially harmful situations is crucial. Practices should encourage self-awareness and respect for one's limits, essential for safety and psychological well-being. This guarantees that personal development takes place in a safe and encouraging setting. A balanced approach to opportunities and difficulties is encouraged by acknowledging and respecting these boundaries. Fostering a respectful mindset toward one's own needs and boundaries is crucial, as is establishing a safe environment for development without worrying about moving beyond one's comfort zone. To build solid personal and professional connections and preserve well-being, this technique promotes good communication and self-respect.

5. Excessive Ruminations

Focusing too much on past events can hinder current emotional well-being and future growth. Learning from the past is important without allowing it to dominate present experiences. Practices should promote living in the now, making plans for the future, and preserving a balanced view of the past. Overcoming the past enables a more proactive and involved way of living. A person's mental health can significantly improve by turning their attention from past mistakes to present chances. This can also help establish an adaptable, forward-looking attitude, which is essential for personal growth. This approach also aids in breaking cycles of negative thinking and promotes a more optimistic and solution-oriented outlook, which is essential for personal fulfillment and success.

6. Materialistic Focus

Practices that emphasize material success or appearances as primary indicators of self-worth can skew perceptions of value and success. Focusing on intrinsic qualities such as kindness, integrity, and creativity promotes a more fulfilling and grounded sense of self that is not dependent on external factors. This focus on internal growth cultivates a rich sense of self that transcends material conditions.

Valuing personal qualities over material achievements fosters deeper satisfaction and a stable sense of self-worth, protecting against the fluctuations of external circumstances. This shift encourages a more meaningful engagement with life, where personal and ethical values drive actions and choices rather than external pressures or material desires.

7. Dependency on External Validation

Seeking external validation can undermine self-confidence and independence. Practices should foster inner validation and self-reliance, enhancing personal empowerment and self-assurance. This helps individuals feel secure in their values and decisions, independent of outside approval. Building a strong internal foundation supports enduring self-esteem and fulfillment. Cultivating self-validation is crucial for emotional independence, reducing the impact of external opinions, and enhancing personal agency and self-esteem.

This empowers individuals to pursue their true interests and passions without being swayed by the expectations or judgments of others, leading to a more authentic and satisfying life.

8. Neglecting Emotional Needs

It is unhealthy to ignore or suppress emotional needs. Effective practices should address and validate these needs, promoting emotional health and resilience. Acknowledging and addressing emotions directly supports overall mental health and interpersonal relationships.

This comprehensive emotional awareness enhances coping strategies and promotes emotional intelligence.

Properly addressing and integrating emotional experiences into daily life can significantly improve overall happiness and stability, preventing emotional suppression that often leads to more significant issues.

This practice fosters a deeper understanding of oneself and others, improving empathy and emotional connectivity, vital for personal relationships and professional success.

9. Forced Positivity

Insisting on constant positivity can invalidate genuine feelings of sadness, frustration, or disappointment. Practices should allow space for all emotions, facilitating a genuine and balanced emotional life. This realism in emotional expression is key to authentic living and well-being. Accepting the whole range of emotions enhances experiences in life and promotes strong mental health. A deeper awareness of one's emotional landscape and increased emotional resilience might result from genuinely allowing oneself to experience and express a wide range of emotions. Emotional honesty leads to better coping strategies and deeper interpersonal bonds, improving interactions with others and overall happiness.

10. Ignoring Physical Limits

It is important to ensure that physical activities are carried out in a way that respects the body's limitations. This helps to prevent injuries and promotes long-term health. Practices should encourage listening to one's body and adjusting activities to accommodate individual physical conditions and capabilities, promoting sustainable physical activity. This prevents physical harm, improves enjoyment, and ensures longevity in physical pursuits. Recognizing and adhering to physical boundaries ensures safety and enhances the effectiveness of physical endeavors, fostering a healthier and more enjoyable relationship with one's body. This respectful approach to physical activity encourages a lifelong engagement with health-promoting behaviors and supports overall well-being.

11. Cult-Like Followings

Avoid practices that demand blind allegiance or suppress individual thought. Healthy practices encourage critical thinking and personal identity, fostering a sense of community while respecting individuality.

This balance supports both personal and communal growth without compromising personal autonomy.

Cultivating an environment of open dialogue and respect for diverse perspectives strengthens the community and individual integrity.

Encouraging independence of thought in communal settings fosters a vibrant and dynamic group dynamic where innovation and personal growth can flourish.

This openness enriches personal experiences and communal interactions, fostering a nurturing environment conducive to personal discovery and collective advancement.

12. Reliance on Material Wealth

Focusing primarily on material wealth or appearances as key indicators of self-worth can distort perceptions of value and success. Emphasizing internal attributes such as compassion, honesty, and creativity fosters a more fulfilling and well-grounded sense of self that is independent of external factors.

This emphasis on internal development nurtures a profound sense of identity that surpasses material conditions. Prioritizing personal qualities over material accomplishments leads to deeper contentment and a stable sense of self-worth, safeguarding against the variations of external situations. This shift fosters a more meaningful engagement with life, where personal and ethical values guide actions and choices instead of external pressures or material desires.

13. Seeking External Approval

Relying on external approval can erode self-confidence and autonomy. Practices should cultivate self-endorsement and self-sufficiency, boosting personal empowerment and confidence. This makes individuals feel secure in their convictions and choices, regardless of external feedback. Developing a robust internal foundation enhances lasting self-worth and satisfaction. Promoting self-endorsement is essential for emotional independence, reducing the influence of external perceptions, and improving personal authority and self-respect. This empowerment allows individuals to follow their genuine interests and aspirations without being influenced by the expectations or judgments of others, leading to a more authentic and gratifying life.

14. Disregarding Emotional Wellness

Overlooking or minimizing emotional needs is detrimental to health. Practices should recognize and affirm these needs, promoting emotional well-being and resilience. Addressing emotions directly supports overall mental health and enriches interpersonal relationships. This thorough emotional awareness enhances coping mechanisms and fosters emotional intelligence. Properly acknowledging and integrating emotional experiences into daily life can significantly elevate happiness and stability, preventing the emotional repression that often leads to more significant issues. This approach cultivates a deeper understanding of one self and others, improving empathy and emotional connectivity, essential for personal relationships and professional success.

15. Unqualified Guidance

Listening to advice from unqualified individuals can result in ineffective or harmful practices. Ensuring that guidance comes from qualified sources is crucial for safety and effectiveness, as well as providing reliable and informed practices that truly benefit personal development. Expert advice is indispensable for achieving significant and safe progress in any practice, reinforcing the value of credible and experienced guidance. Seeking out well-qualified leaders or mentors not only enhances the quality of guidance received but also secures the safety and efficacy of the practices undertaken. This commitment to high standards of leadership and instruction guarantees that personal and professional development is both meaningful and beneficial, laying a solid foundation for lifelong learning and growth.

In essence, by shifting focus from material success and external validation to fostering intrinsic qualities and emotional well-being, individuals can cultivate a more authentic and fulfilling life. This approach enables a stable sense of self-worth based on personal values and ethical choices, independent of external circumstances. This allows for a more meaningful engagement with life. Addressing emotional needs and allowing for a genuine expression of all emotions further supports mental health and interpersonal relationships, enhancing personal resilience and emotional intelligence. Such practices not only prevent the adverse effects of materialistic focus and forced positivity but also promote a healthy, balanced lifestyle that prioritizes personal growth and well-being over superficial metrics of success. This comprehensive approach leads to deeper personal satisfaction, improved relationships, and a more purposeful life.

Chapter 4: Illuminating the Path - Finding Your Inner Light

"Knowing yourself is the beginning of all wisdom."

-Aristotle.

Moving from darkness to light powerfully captures our journey toward self-discovery and spiritual awakening. This journey is akin to emerging from a shadowy, unclear path into a brightly lit road where every detail is discernible. It signifies the transition from ignorance and confusion to clarity and enlightenment, both literally and metaphorically.

As this transformation unfolds, it often brings a series of revelations and realizations that challenge our former selves and urge us to evolve. Each step forward on this path not only enlightens us but also empowers us to guide others who might still be searching in the shadows.

In the early stages of life, many of us operate under layers of societal conditioning and personal biases that cloud our true nature and potential. This phase can be likened to being in the dark, where our vision is obscured, and our paths are uncertain. We might stumble, make mistakes, and feel lost, much as one would in a physically dark environment.

Yet, in these moments of uncertainty and missteps, our resilience is tested, and our desire to seek the light strengthens. Overcoming these challenges stands as proof of our capacity for growth and adaptability, opening us up to new possibilities and paths. As we search for deeper comprehension, we often encounter moments that challenge our assumptions and compel us to question our firmly held views. These are the initial glimmers of light—instances of realization that, though brief, start to illuminate our environment. Engaging with varying viewpoints, encountering life's diverse circumstances, and pondering our responses aid in progressively brightening the obscure areas of our comprehension. This slow enlightenment nurtures a setting where education and development are cherished, encouraging us to stay open and responsive to the transformative influence of newfound knowledge.

The pursuit of knowledge is essential in this transformative journey. It involves actively seeking out experiences and wisdom that broaden our horizons. Just as dawn slowly dispels the night with its gentle light, acquiring knowledge helps dispel ignorance, lighting our minds and spirits. This knowledge is derived from our own experiences, books, and lectures. As we gain new understanding, our perspective broadens, and we live more fully. This constant process of learning not only improves our quality of life but also enables us to better meet obstacles in the future.

However, this path is not without its obstacles. When new realities contradict our preconceived notions, we, too, need to adapt our inner selves, much as we must adjust our eyes to a quick flash of light after being in the dark.

It is an essential component of development, even if it can be unpleasant or even painful. Every step we take in the direction of the light improves our capacity for better vision and more purposeful and intentional life navigation. These changes lessen in shock as we go along and increasingly become a part of our ongoing development, which reflects our dedication to growth and development. A proverb says, *"A smooth sea never made a skilled sailor."* This serves as a reminder that we actually develop and learn best when we overcome obstacles and adjust to change.

The concept of self-awareness looms larger as we proceed along this route. Like light itself, self-awareness enables us to perceive what is inside as well as outside of ourselves. Real progress necessitates a more profound level of introspection and authenticity, which it encourages.

As we become more conscious of ourselves, we start to recognize the origins of our ideas and actions and can tell which are really our own and which are forced by other factors. This increased awareness has a transforming power that enables us to act ethically and authentically in accordance with our core ideals.

This heightened self-awareness leads to stronger control over our reactions, emotions, and ideas because we are no longer reacting instinctively from a position of darkness (ignorance) but are making conscious decisions based on the light of our new understanding. This control is not about suppression or denial but about making educated decisions that fit with our genuine selves. As we master this control, we become architects of our fate, capable of creating our destiny in ways that reflect our highest desires and deepest understandings.

Moreover, this journey shapes our relationships. As we walk toward the light, our relationships can either change with us or become hard. We may find that our interactions with others also need to adapt as we evolve. Some relationships may strengthen, while others may slip away, much like leaves shedding from a tree in autumn. This is a normal and healthy process as it clears space for more honest interactions that resonate with our new path. Going through these changes demands knowledge and compassion, both for ourselves and for others around us, as everyone is on their own unique journey.

The quest for light also often leads us into the service of others. As our journey progresses, the insights and wisdom we receive frequently inspire a natural desire to help others find their way out of the darkness. This service does not necessarily entail huge actions but can emerge in little acts of compassion, giving knowledge, or offering a listening ear. In assisting others, we spread the light and deepen our awareness and commitment to this road. Our lights shine brightest when shared, and through service, we learn the genuine meaning of community and interconnection.

Moving from darkness to light becomes more about living intentionally and purposefully on a daily basis than it does about arriving at a destination. It is a never-ending process of learning, developing, and enlightening—for the outside world as well. Every step offers fresh insights, difficulties, and chances for greater understanding and connection; this always-changing journey is what keeps the route intriguing and rewarding. As we continue on our own paths of illumination and discovery, we also serve as beacons of light for those who come after us.

Consider the story of Malika, a young lady who grew up in a small, conservative town where conventional duties and expectations were deeply instilled. From a young age, Malika was encouraged to conform to these norms without question. However, as she grew older, she began to experience a contradiction between her community's values and her own emerging beliefs. The gloom of confusion and uniformity was all she knew until she decided to pursue higher education abroad.

This decision was her first step into the light. Immersed in a new environment, Malika experienced numerous cultures and philosophies that starkly contrasted with her upbringing. Each lecture, each debate with peers, was like a ray of light breaking through the darkness of her previous view of the universe.

This exposure was not without obstacles; there were times of self-doubt and cultural shock, analogous to the discomfort one feels when walking into strong sunlight after long hours in the dark. Yet, these hurdles became stepping stones for Malika to develop a stronger, more real personality over time. Her fortitude in the face of these problems shows the transformative power of accepting and using the unknown as a catalyst for personal progress.

Through education and interaction, Malika obtained insights that brightened her mind and soul. She learned to question, evaluate, and, most importantly, understand herself independently from her cultural upbringing.

This path of moving from darkness to light transformed Malika, enabling her to return to her community not just with new knowledge but also with a new vision to contribute positively and motivate others to seek their light. Her transformation highlights how enlightenment may reach beyond the individual, impacting groups and cultures by bringing new ideas and possibilities. This example shows how transitioning from ignorance to knowledge can deeply impact one's existence.

It highlights the profound change in outlook and way of life that can occur when one escapes the shadows of unawareness and moves toward the light of comprehension and self-awareness. Malika's story emphasizes the impact that insight and self-discovery can have on one self and as a source of transformation and enlightenment for others around them.

Discovering and Living by One's Unique Purpose

Based on the foundational insights, let's delve deeper into the journey of discovering and living by one's unique purpose and inner truth—a journey that significantly impacts an individual's life. This process involves a deep exploration of one's core values and passions, leading to an understanding of One's true self.

The discovery and subsequent embrace of this inner truth can trigger a chain of positive transformations, bringing a profound sense of satisfaction, purpose, and peace that touches every facet of life.

This journey is not just about personal growth but a complete shift, empowering individuals to live lives that align with their core values and aspirations. Friedrich Nietzsche, a German philosopher, captures this sentiment perfectly, saying, *"He who has a why to live can bear almost any how."* This quote highlights the empowering nature of having a purpose, which not only guides but also strengthens individuals through life's challenges. Below are the stages and impacts of the journey toward discovering and living by one's unique purpose and inner truth:

self-assurance and inner tranquility. One's quest toward self-actualization is reinforced by this newfound congruence between one's inner and outside worlds, which results in a harmonious existence that radiates positivity and draws similar energy.

Impact on Personal and Professional Life

Finding and living one's purpose has significant and far-reaching consequences. People feel more content and comfortable on a personal level. As a result of their more sincere and empathetic interactions with others, they form healthier connections. They experience more success and fulfillment in their careers. They find drive and joy in their work, which frequently results in creativity and excellence when they match their career with their actual passions. Thus, this connection is a strong motivator for both professional and personal development. It gives people the opportunity to contribute to the fullest extent possible, adding value in ways that profoundly align with their values and career goals.

Broader Social Impact

Living one's truth has a greater social influence than just in the personal and professional spheres. People who are in sync with their inner purpose frequently serve as an inspiration to people around them. They serve as inspirations, demonstrating to others that leading a satisfying and genuine life is achievable. Furthermore, numerous individuals discover ways to positively impact society—whether through their professional endeavors, volunteering or by promoting empathy and compassion in their everyday interactions. This wider influence shows how leading an authentic life has a domino effect, meaningfully impacting communities and societies. By sharing their experiences, these people encourage others to start their own journeys of self-discovery, resulting in a circle of development and transformation that goes beyond personal experiences.

The Continuous Journey

Following one's inner truth is a constant journey rather than a final destination. It requires ongoing introspection and adjustment as one grows and experiences changes in one's environment. Being faithful to oneself is a continuous process that needs effort and attention. One can stay in tune with their changing self through this ongoing adaptation, which makes life an ongoing learning and development process. Accepting this continuous process makes it possible for people to remain open to opportunities and challenges, making their lives continuously rich in learning and development.

The journey toward discovering and living by one's unique purpose and inner truth is one of the most significant undertakings a person can embark on. It transforms lives, providing not only personal fulfillment and peace but also making a lasting impact on society. This path, rich with personal development and discovery, is essential for anyone seeking a meaningful and impactful existence. It demonstrates that true happiness and success lie in understanding and aligning with one's deepest values and passions.

Simple Spiritual Practices to Uncover and Nurture Inner Light

Engaging in spiritual practices is a transformative process that enhances self-awareness and fosters a connection with the deeper aspects of one's being. These practices help individuals connect with their inner wisdom and emotional depths, acting as gateways to personal enlightenment and spiritual growth. Integrating these rituals into daily life can cultivate a harmonious balance between the mind, body, and spirit, leading to a more centered and peaceful existence. Here are 15 simple practices that can help individuals illuminate and nurture the light within, leading to increased peace, balance, and fulfillment in their lives.

Each practice, when performed consistently, serves as a tool for self-discovery and mental clarity, ultimately enhancing one's overall quality of life and interactions with others.

1. Mindfulness Meditation:

Mindfulness meditation involves sitting quietly and paying attention to thoughts, sounds, the sensations of breathing, or parts of the body. It's a practice that helps bring about a state of calm and awareness in the present moment. Regular mindfulness meditation can reduce stress, enhance concentration, and contribute to a greater sense of control in one's life. Over time, it fosters a deepened awareness of the mind-body connection and can help one manage anxiety more effectively.

This practice also supports emotional resilience, enabling individuals to respond to life's challenges with more grace and less reactivity. It teaches patience and acceptance, key qualities that improve personal interactions and decision-making.

2. Gratitude Reflection:

Engaging in gratitude reflection means actively recognizing things one appreciates, from minor delights to major joys. This practice can alter perspectives from focusing on lacking to appreciating abundance, effectively boosting happiness and contentment. By acknowledging and valuing the positive, individuals can build resilience against pessimistic thoughts and improve their overall mental health. Daily gratitude reflection promotes a positive mindset and fosters a general feeling of satisfaction and well-being, easing the handling of difficult times. It also strengthens relationships by encouraging appreciation for others and fostering positive social exchanges.

3. Reading Spiritual Texts:

Diving into spiritual writings can offer philosophical insights and moral guidance. This practice opens new paths for personal contemplation and insight, allowing individuals to delve into spiritual traditions and wisdom from diverse cultures and times.

Whether it's sacred texts, profound teachings, or philosophical discussions, these texts deepen one's connection to the broader human journey and the divine. Regular reading of these materials can also enhance one's empathy and understanding of others, promoting a more empathetic worldview. It provides a sense of tranquility and stability, grounding individuals in the wisdom that goes beyond daily challenges and uncertainties.

4. Guided Visualizations:

Guided visualizations involve following a spoken narrative to imagine a relaxing scene or journey. This technique can be very useful for reaching particular life objectives or enhancing health because it lowers stress. It encourages relaxation and makes significant psychological shifts possible by positively and intently engaging the mind. A powerful technique for self-motivation, visualization enables one to intentionally and clearly see the desired result to help bring goals to life. By strengthening mental resilience, this approach enables people to approach obstacles with a focused and clear perspective.

5. Breathwork:

Using a range of breathing practices, breathwork aims to enhance one's physical, mental, and spiritual health. Practices like regulated breathing can lower blood pressure, encourage serenity, and maintain emotional stability. This technique improves emotional regulation and self-awareness by building a connection between the conscious and subconscious minds. Depending on the approach, it can also invigorate the body or encourage relaxation, giving it a flexible tool for handling daily stressors and emotional states. Additionally, it facilitates the integration of mental and physical healing, offering a very effective and approachable holistic approach to wellness.

6. Art Therapy:

Through creative self-expression, people can discover and work through emotional issues. This practice offers a means of examining inner emotions, growing self-awareness, controlling behavior, lowering anxiety, and raising self-esteem. Those who struggle to communicate their ideas and feelings vocally will find it especially helpful. Art therapy has applications in schools and rehabilitation centers, and it can help people of all ages. It encourages creative problem-solving and an emotional release that may be rather liberating and empowering.

7. Tai Chi or Qigong:

These age-old Chinese practices blend focused mental attention and regulated breathing with slow, purposeful motion. Stress and anxiety are well-recognized to be reduced by tai chi and qigong, which also enhance strength, agility, and balance. Frequent practice offers a tranquil environment for reflection and meditation as well as enhancement of general health. Together with encouraging lifespan, these activities help people mature with greater mental and physical agility. In groups, they also foster a sense of connectedness and community, which enhances social as well as physical and mental health.

8. Digital Detox:

A digital detox is a certain amount of time spent not using computers, tablets, or cell phones. Stress reduction, real-world relationship building, and an active lifestyle are all facilitated by this practice. It exhorts people to reconnect with themselves away from digital distractions and to interact more fully with their physical environment. Regular digital detoxification can lengthen attention span, lower anxiety, and improve the quality of sleep. In addition, it promotes awareness and presence— qualities that are sometimes weakened by continual connection.

9. Aromatherapy:

Aromatherapy uses essential oils extracted from plants to enhance psychological and physical well-being. Diffusing oils into the air, ingesting them straight, or massaging them into the skin are possible.

Different therapeutic qualities of each essential oil can help to balance, excite, or calm the body and mind. This natural healing method can enhance other treatments and promote overall well-being by aligning physical, mental, and emotional health.

Additionally, aromatherapy offers a sensory experience that can instantly improve mood and establish a soothing environment, and it is a great stress-reduction technique.

10. Sacred Space Creation:

Creating a sacred space is about designating a physical area for spiritual activities like meditation, prayer, or reflection. This designated area becomes a private haven that promotes spiritual activities by offering a place to concentrate on introspection and inner serenity.

Maintaining a daily spiritual practice, which can be crucial for long-term spiritual growth, can be made simpler with a sacred space at home. Additionally, it gives daily routines a ritualistic and significant touch that strengthens one's dedication to spiritual development and increases their influence.

11. Mindful Walking:

Mindful walking is practicing mindfulness while walking. It involves noticing the movement of the body, the sensation of feet touching the ground, the sounds in the environment, and the breathing. This practice helps connect the body and mind, grounding the practitioner in the present moment and promoting serenity.

It can be especially beneficial in natural environments, where being in touch with the natural world can deepen the meditative experience. Moreover, mindful walking promotes physical health by increasing flexibility and circulation. As such, it is a complete practice that enhances total well-being.

12. Mantra Chanting:

To focus the mind and uplift the spirit, chanting mantras entails repeating a series of phrases or sounds. A deeper state of meditation is often attained through this practice. Mantras are frequently taken from spiritual or religious books and can be extremely traditional or deeply personal. Chanting's vibrational qualities can soothe the body and mind and promote a very tranquil state of inner silence. Moreover, it supports the development of a regular breathing pattern that improves both mental and physical clarity and relaxation.

13. Herbal Tea Rituals:

Herbal tea rituals include choosing, preparing, and drinking herbal tea with awareness. This practice promotes introspection and relaxation. A peaceful period during a hectic day can be fostered by the ritual of making and drinking tea, which has various health advantages depending on the variety of herbal tea. This practice can act as a daily reminder to decelerate and appreciate the here and now. It also offers a gentle approach to incorporating healthful herbs into a diet, which can help with physical health in a number of ways.

14. Daily Reflection:

Devoting some time each day to contemplate your deeds, choices, and feelings can result in a more profound understanding of yourself and more thoughtful life decisions. This practice can help you understand your personal patterns and motivations, leading to greater self-awareness and intentional living. It's a chance to consider the impacts of your behavior and to align your daily actions with your larger life goals. Daily reflection fosters perspective and patience, two qualities essential to human growth. It also offers a chance to modify how one approaches obstacles and successes, encouraging ongoing personal development.

15. Volunteering and Acts of Kindness:

Engaging in volunteer work and performing random acts of kindness can help shift our focus from ourselves to others, promoting empathy and social connection. This practice can lead to a greater sense of purpose and happiness, not only in the lives of those we help but also in our own lives, by providing a sense of fulfillment and connectedness. Regularly engaging in altruistic endeavors can result in long-term changes to our perspective of the world and our place in it, which often leads to increased life satisfaction and reduced feelings of loneliness. Furthermore, by doing these things, we can strengthen communities and foster a culture of kindness and support.

Therefore, participating in spiritual practices not only nourishes one's inner being but also enhances connections with the surrounding environment. These diverse practices provide resources to help individuals gain a greater understanding of themselves and build meaningful relationships with others, ultimately improving overall life satisfaction and emotional well-being. Whether through various practices like meditation, expressing gratitude, or setting up special spaces, each method can bring about meaningful personal development and satisfaction. As these practices become ingrained in daily life, they foster the development of a more compassionate, balanced, and aware existence, proving that the path to spiritual enlightenment is both enlightening and life-changing. People who adopt these practices can experience a great sense of balance and serenity in their lives, as well as genuinely light the deeper sides of themselves.

Stories of Inspiration and Hope Through Self-Discovery

Over the course of human history, numerous individuals have undertaken transformative journeys of self-exploration, which have imbued their lives with inspiration and optimism for those around them.

These stories exemplify the tenacity and strength of the human spirit and underscore how individual development can affect one's own existence and that of others.

Here, let's explore several inspiring stories that demonstrate the transformative power of embracing personal challenges and insights. The journey toward self-discovery often begins with a pivotal moment of challenge or crisis, igniting a quest for deeper understanding and meaning in life.

1. Liz Murray: From Homeless to Harvard

Liz Murray's life story is a powerful example of overcoming extreme adversity through determination and education. Growing up in the Bronx with drug-addicted parents, Murray faced homelessness at a young age. Despite these challenges, she remained focused on her education, eventually earning a scholarship to Harvard University.

Her memoir, "Breaking Night," chronicles her journey from the streets to one of the world's most prestigious universities, offering hope and motivation to those facing similar hardships. Murray's life underlines the transformative power of perseverance and education, inspiring many to strive for their dreams despite seemingly insurmountable obstacles.

2. Stephen Hawking: Defying Limits through Intellectual Brilliance

Stephen Hawking was diagnosed with a motor neuron disease when he was 21 and was given just a few years to live. However, he defied all odds and became one of the most renowned theoretical physicists of his time. His contributions expanded our knowledge of black holes and the cosmos and inspired people to investigate difficult scientific concepts and overcome personal obstacles. Hawking was known for his tenacity and ability to explain complex scientific ideas in an accessible way to the general public, making cosmology and physics more interesting and approachable to a worldwide audience. His determination is a testament to the human spirit's ability to achieve greatness and overcome apparent limitations.

3. Maya Angelou: Literary Voice of Justice and Equality

Maya Angelou, an American poet and civil rights activist, turned her painful early experiences of personal trauma and racial injustice to inspire many others to seek justice and equality through her potent literary works and public speeches. Her efforts have come to represent resiliency and strength, especially in the Black community. Her persuasive writings and expressive voice never cease to move audiences as she speaks out in favor of social fairness and moral rectitude. Angelou's lasting impact shows how the arts can be a transforming force for both social progress and individual healing.

4. Christopher Reeve: Turning Tragedy into Activism

Best known for his role as Superman, Christopher Reeve became a quadriplegic following a horse-riding accident. He turned this personal sorrow into a motivation to advocate, giving his life to disability rights and spinal cord research. His charity has made major research funding and quality-of-life improvements for paralyzed individuals possible, demonstrating how individual hardship may spur social support and beneficial change. Reeve's legacy serves as a powerful reminder of the positive social impact that one person's determination can have, encouraging people to support social change and further scientific and medical research.

5.   J.K. Rowling: Crafting Worlds from the Brink of Despair

J.K. Rowling's transformation from a struggling single mother living on welfare to the author of the bestselling Harry Potter series is a remarkable story of perseverance. The world of Hogwarts not only enchanted readers worldwide but also provided hope and a sense of belonging to many. Rowling's journey is a powerful reminder of how creativity can emerge from hardship and lead to widespread impact, both literary and charitable. Her narrative encourages us to believe in the redemptive power of stories, affirming that one's darkest moments can lead to the brightest futures.

6.   Sheryl Sandberg: Turning Grief into Action

After the sudden death of her husband, Sheryl Sandberg, the COO of Facebook, faced profound grief that reshaped her perspective on work and life. As a co-author, she delves into the themes of rehabilitation and resilience in her post-loss book "Option B," which provides advice on how to face hardship and loss. Sandberg's story exemplifies how one's own suffering can lead to activism and solidarity with those going through tough times. Her story has shed light on the power of perseverance and healing in the face of adversity, helping others to comprehend the role of loss in individuals better

7.   Jane Goodall: Pioneering Conservation and Empathy for Wildlife

Jane Goodall's groundbreaking work with chimpanzees in Tanzania provides profound insights into primates' emotional world, highlighting the deep connections between humans and animals. Starting with little more than a notebook and binoculars, Goodall challenged scientific norms and revolutionized primatology by demonstrating that chimpanzees have personalities and complex social relationships. Her enduring dedication to wild life conservation and her advocacy for sustainable living continue to inspire a global audience to respect and protect the natural world. Good all's journey shows the power of passion and perseverance in sparking global conversations about conservation and animal welfare.

Every one of these people has a story that shows their resilience and ability to overcome adversity and how such changes can encourage and uplift others. They have shown that personal development may have a significant impact on and ignite larger societal change by overcoming obstacles and sharing their knowledge. Through their experiences, we are reminded of the limitless potential that every person possesses to change not only their own life but also the world around them.

Chapter 5: Cultivating Compassion - For Self and Others

"Be kind, for everyone you meet is fighting a hard battle."

-Ian Maclaren

Growing compassion, both for ourselves and others, plays a crucial role in our journey toward spiritual and personal development. This evolution involves not only feeling more empathy and kindness toward others but also understanding and forgiving ourselves.

It involves recognizing our own struggles and those of others with a kind heart, thereby fostering a deeper connection to the human experience. Through this understanding, we become more attuned to the subtleties of emotional distress and more capable of genuine support. Practicing compassion enhances our ability to empathize and enriches the quality of our connections, creating a more caring community.

Compassion is essentially the emotional response where one feels moved by another's suffering and desires to help alleviate it. It goes further than simple empathy, which entails grasping someone else's viewpoint or emotions.

Compassion drives us to act to help those in hardship. Take, for example, a community volunteer who attentively hears the hardships faced by older inhabitants and arranges extra aid and resources for them. This change starts from within; we can't fully comprehend or help others until we've reconciled our own internal struggles and dilemmas. By nurturing this inner compassion, we lay a solid foundation for external acts of kindness. Thus, compassion stands as both a personal endeavor and a social skill, enhancing our interactions and interventions in times of need. Practicing self-compassion is treating oneself with the same decency and consideration that one would extend to a close friend. This calls for accepting and being kind to oneself when one is hurting, failing, or feeling inadequate rather than ignoring our sorrow or punishing ourselves with condemnation of oneself.

Self-care also involves acknowledging that experiencing suffering and personal shortcomings are part of the universal human condition—common to us all rather than unique to us individually. This recognition is crucial for mental well-being and personal growth, as it equips us to manage life's obstacles gracefully. Moreover, it reduces the detrimental effects of stress and anxiety, encouraging a more balanced and forgiving perspective of oneself.

The practice of developing compassion can be transformative. It helps us to communicate with people more genuinely and, by bringing to light our shared human experiences, reduces feelings of loneliness. It also gives us the ability to manage trying circumstances better since it builds emotional resilience.

Developing a compassionate attitude helps us become less critical of both ourselves and other people and more accepting. Developing deep relationships and a network of support requires this shift in viewpoint. It contributes to a healthier social setting where collective welfare is cherished and fostered. The widespread impact of such changes can greatly reduce social tensions and encourage a more peaceful coexistence. Moreover, compassion has significant spiritual implications. The value of compassion is emphasized by numerous spiritual traditions all over the world as a way to transcend the self and establish a connection with a greater purpose.

These traditions view compassion as a condition of being that represents a deep understanding of the interconnection of all life, as well as a road to spiritual enlightenment. Accepting this interconnection inspires us to coexist more peacefully with the natural world and all living things. This viewpoint encourages a deeper respect for life in all of its forms and points us in the direction of more thoughtful and sustainable actions.

We begin to observe a ripple effect in our environment as we cultivate compassion within ourselves. Our relationships soften, our hearts widen, and our actions more closely reflect our ideals of compassion and understanding. This does not imply that challenges or conflicts will disappear from our lives; rather, it means that we will have a wider range of emotional tools at our disposal to handle them.

These tools improve our capacity to endure hardship and foster harmony and comprehension in a variety of contexts. As we keep developing these traits, we light up our communities as sources of solace and resilience, encouraging others to follow in our footsteps and become more compassionate people.

True compassion is a lifetime journey to develop. It calls for constant practice and learning. It begins with little steps, like pausing in a painful or frustrating time to take a deep breath and treat ourselves with love. These small deeds of kindness add up over time, changing our perception of ourselves and the way we engage with the outside world. Every step we take on this road enhances our relationships and increases our sense of fulfillment in life. This path not only makes us into more compassionate people but also changes our surroundings into welcoming and nurturing places.

Learning more about the experiences and lives of others is another way that we might increase our capacity for compassion. Books, videos, talks, and encounters with other cultures and systems can all contribute to this knowledge.

By tearing down barriers and preconceptions, this deeper comprehension increases our empathy and decreases our propensity to cause harm to others by ignorance or misinterpretation. Thus, education serves as a bridge that unites people from different backgrounds and promotes an understanding and respectful global community. It also gives us the intelligence and empathy to recognize and address the various challenges that people around us encounter.

Furthermore, practicing regular mindfulness and self-awareness exercises like yoga, writing, or meditation can improve our capacity to be in the moment and responsive to the pain of others. These practices support us in controlling our own stress and emotional responses, which are critical abilities for preserving compassion in trying circumstances.

Regular engagement in these practices fosters mental clarity and calmness, which significantly increases our capacity for compassion and empathy. They also enable us to avoid burnout and preserve our mental well-being, which guarantees our capacity to support others effectively in the future. Community involvement is another vital aspect of developing compassion. By participating in community service or group activities aimed at helping others, we can directly experience the impact of collective compassionate action. These experiences not only provide immediate benefits to those helped but also deepen our own feelings of connection and purpose.

They also teach us about the practical aspects of implementing compassionate solutions in real-world scenarios, thus grounding our theoretical knowledge in lived experience. Engaging in such activities reinforces our commitment to compassion and enhances our skills in collaborative and empathetic problem-solving.

Teaching compassion and empathy from a young age is imperative. Families and schools are essential in this because they set an example of compassion and reinforce it. Children who are raised to be considerate of others' feelings and to act kindly toward them are likely to develop into adults who make valuable contributions to both their local communities and the larger world.

The saying *"A tree is bent while it is young"* emphasizes the need to form behavior early in life. Early instillation of these principles helps to reduce conflict and create a more united community by preparing future generations to face the world with empathy. Teaching young individuals about empathy ensures the continuation of these vital principles, leading to a more understanding and peaceful society. The growth of compassion is a key component of spiritual and personal growth. It bolsters our emotional sturdiness, improves our interactions, and boosts our overall health. As we become more empathetic, we not only better our own circumstances but also aid in creating a more understanding world. Through education, regular practice, and active participation in community activities, we can further develop our ability for empathy, making it a central element of our daily lives and exchanges. This continuous effort benefits us on a personal level and has a profound impact on the social structure, nurturing a culture of kindness and consideration. Along with helping each of us personally, this continuous process affects society as a whole and promotes a respectful and caring culture.

Cultivating Compassion through Simple Meditation Practices

Practices in meditation help us to grow a more kind and understanding heart toward ourselves, which naturally carries over to other people. This guide offers simple meditation exercises to help you develop compassion in your day-to-day activities so that you may be nice to people around you as well. Regular meditation not only lowers stress and increases mental clarity but also increases emotional awareness, which is essential for developing compassion.

Here's the list of meditation practices:

1. Basic Breathing Meditation for Self-Compassion

Exercise:

Start by finding a quiet place where you won't be disturbed. Close your eyes, choose a comfortable spot to sit, and start concentrating only on your breathing. Breathe gently out of your mouth after taking a deep breath through your nose, which causes your belly and chest to lift. Visualize letting go of any negative or self-judgmental feelings as you exhale. Feel the warmth leaving as the air rises and falls, and let this process happen slowly.

Purpose:

This exercise is designed to ground you in the present moment and reduce stress, making it easier to address yourself with kindness. By concentrating on each breath, you allow yourself to connect with the present moment, a fundamental step in developing self-compassion. By repeatedly focusing on the breath, one can break the pattern of self-criticism and negative thoughts, promoting acceptance and tranquility. Regular practice helps foster a nurturing attitude toward yourself and greatly improves your emotional resilience.

2. Loving-Kindness Meditation (Metta)

Exercise:

Beginning while you're still in a relaxed sitting position, say positive affirmations to yourself aloud, like "May I be happy, may I be healthy, may I be safe, may I live with ease." Once a few minutes have passed, expand these ideas to include someone you love, someone you feel neutral toward, and even someone you find difficult. Imagine that every single person gets your best wishes and has a happy moment.

Purpose:

Loving-kindness meditation is used to foster a sense of benevolence and care first toward oneself and then toward others. This practice gradually incorporates all beings into your circle of love, which helps dissolve barriers to compassion. By saying these a loud, one develops a loving and forgiving mindset that grows from them to include others in a never-ending circle of compassion. This meditation can gradually change your perspective and foster more harmony and understanding in your relationships.

3. Compassion Visualization

Exercise:

Imagine a loved one going through a difficult time. Try to visualize them as clearly as you can, and consider the stress or suffering they may be going through. Imagine now that a soft, comforting light is coming from your heart, reaching out to them and taking away their suffering. Feel the warmth of your heart guiding them, motivated by your desire for their well-being. Imagine their relief and the peace that follows to enhance this visualization further.

Purpose:

This exercise aids you in not only empathizing with others but also in actively hoping for their freedom from distress. It fortifies the emotional ties you experience, rendering your acts of kindness more heartfelt and authentic. Compassion can go beyond just being a sentiment and become a powerful force that strengthens your emotional connections with others and enables you to offer comfort. By regularly practicing compassion, you can improve your ability to respond to the needs of others with empathy and action. The use of imagery can be particularly helpful in cultivating this habit and enhancing your capacity to connect with others.

4. Mindfulness Walk

Exercise:

Choose a natural setting for a quiet walk, such as a park or a garden. As you proceed, focus intently on the feelings beneath your feet, the noises surrounding you, and the breeze moving against your skin. When your thoughts drift, softly redirect your focus to the act of walking and breathing. Observe the hues and textures around you, and let each step draw you nearer to a state of mindful awareness.

Purpose:

This practice integrates mindfulness with physical exercise, facilitating a way to remain completely absorbed in the present while fostering a state of vigilant relaxation. Mindfulness walks are excellent for decluttering your mind, diminishing stress, and bolstering your empathy capacity. They offer a distinct chance to engage in mindfulness while in motion, anchoring you in the tangible world while boosting your mental and emotional health. Such walks can serve as a powerful means to nurture a calm and observant mind.

5. Gratitude Reflection

Exercise:

End your day by contemplating three things you appreciate. These might be as simple as an enjoyable cup of coffee, a rewarding conversation, or the coziness of your abode. Truly immerse yourself in the gratitude as you contemplate each element. Aim to pinpoint exactly why you appreciate each aspect, and take note of any feelings of warmth or satisfaction that emerge within you.

Purpose:

Nurturing gratitude is closely connected to compassion. By acknowledging the positives in your life, you shift your attention from negative thought patterns and foster a more optimistic mindset, which boosts your capability to offer kindness and understanding to others. This practice not only elevates your emotional well-being but also lays the ground work for compassion, simplifying the process of connecting with and aiding others. Regular gratitude reflections can significantly influence your overall joy and interpersonal relationships.

6. Focused Compassion Meditation

Exercise:

Find a quiet spot to sit, then close your eyes. Start by concentrating on your body's sensations, particularly around the heart area. Imagine that as you take a breath, your heart becomes larger and brighter. With every breath out, visualize the relief and joy this warmth will bring to a particular person or group that is suffering. As you accomplish this, become aware of the warmth that fills your body from head to toe, strengthening your bond with the individual or group.

Purpose:

The goal of this meditation is to actively transmit positive energy to people to cultivate compassion for them. Fostering a more profound feeling of unity and empathy strengthens the emotional channels that result in empathetic responses in actual circumstances. Regular practice of this meditation enhances your ability to react compassionately in spontaneous situations, which improves your connections with others and your potential to have a beneficial impact on them.

7. Reflection on Interconnectedness

Exercise:

Sit in a peaceful place and reflect on the many ways your life is interconnected with others, from the food you eat to the clothes you wear. Acknowledge how other people have impacted your life, and give them a silent thank you. In order to foster a sense of accountability and concern for your wider impact on the world, this practice might also entail thinking about how your actions affect other people. Extend this contemplation to encompass the global community, considering how even seemingly insignificant actions can have far-reaching effects on individuals worldwide.

Purpose:

This exercise encourages a broader perspective on our place in the world, fostering an understanding of how deeply interconnected our lives are with others. By realizing our interdependence, we naturally cultivate a deeper compassion for the people around us and a greater appreciation for our role in the larger community. This understanding can profoundly shift how we make decisions and interact with the world, fostering a more compassionate and considerate global citizenship.

8. Self-Compassion Break

Exercise:

Whenever you notice you are experiencing a moment of stress or discomfort, take a brief pause. Close your eyes and place a hand on your heart. Remind yourself that suffering is a part of life and say to yourself, "May I be kind to myself in this moment; may I accept this suffering with compassion." Breathe deeply and allow yourself to feel comforted and soothed. Use this moment to give yourself the same kindness and care you would offer a good friend in distress.

Purpose:

This quick practice is essential for cultivating compassion in daily life. It teaches you how to show compassion when you're in need, which helps you incorporate self-compassion into everyday routines. This eases your own pain and makes it easier for you to spontaneously and successfully provide compassion to others. Regular application of this technique can enhance overall mental health and well-being by fostering the development of a resilient and empathetic response to life's adversities. Incorporating these meditation practices into your routine can lead to substantial changes in how you treat yourself and interact with others.

Each exercise is designed to be straightforward and accessible, making it easy to begin the journey toward a more compassionate life. As you continue with these practices, you may find that the kindness you cultivate within yourself naturally flows outward, positively affecting your relationships and overall life approach.

Compassionate Acts: Bridging Divides and Healing Spirits

"Compassion and tolerance are not a sign of weakness, but a sign of strength."

-Dalai Lama.

Here are a few touching accounts of compassion healing spirits and bringing people closer together, highlighting the transformative power of empathy and kindness.

1. A Meal to Mend Fences

In a small rural community rife with political and ideological divisions, a local diner owner decided to host a monthly dinner where people from opposing sides were invited to share a table. The only rule was to leave politics at the door and share personal stories about their lives. Over hearty meals, they discussed families, struggles, and dreams. Over time, these dinners transformed the community's atmosphere. People began seeing each other not as adversaries but as neighbors facing similar challenges. The diner became a symbol of unity, proving that even in times of division, breaking bread together can mend fences and foster a renewed sense of community.

2.   Music for the Soul

In a bustling city marked by fast-paced life and cultural clashes, an elderly musician named Clara used her violin to bring harmony to a fractured neighborhood. Every evening, she played her violin by her window, facing the busy street.

Her beautiful melodies often caused passersby to stop and listen. One evening, during a particularly tense period following a local conflict, Clara's music attracted a large crowd. Moved by the gathering, she invited other local musicians to join her. This impromptu concert sparked a series of musical evenings, becoming a beloved local tradition. Clara's music reminded everyone that beauty and harmony could transcend cultural barriers, bringing solace and connection to a diverse community.

3.   Gardens of Growth

In a marginalized neighborhood plagued by unemployment and neglect, a group of residents transformed an abandoned lot into a community garden. Under the direction of Sofia, a retired teacher, the project swiftly expanded beyond its original goals of regional beautification. People of different ages and backgrounds gathered to plant flowers and vegetables. Residents dismantled barriers to isolation and mistrust by cooperating with one another. People began to gather in the garden as a place of refuge and a way to strengthen their bonds as a community, sharing not just the products of their labor but also their personal anecdotes and encouragement for one another. This green space promoted a feeling of pride and group achievement, demonstrating how common objectives can bring a community together.

4. Letters of Hope

Following a natural disaster that impacted a small coastal town, Mark, a teacher, organized a letter-writing campaign among his students to offer words of encouragement and support to the afflicted individuals. Hundreds of letters from all throughout the region were received as the campaign swiftly expanded beyond the school.

The goodwill of strangers touched the hearts of the recipients of these messages, many of whom had lost everything. Many people experienced emotional relief from this gesture of support, which also started a domino effect of similar actions. It demonstrated how small deeds of kindness, like sending a letter, may bring great consolation and a sense of group resilience when faced with hardship.

5. Lights of Guidance

In a city facing high rates of youth delinquency and crime, a retired police officer named Luis initiated a mentoring program called "Lights of Guidance." His idea, which was straightforward but effective, was to match mentors who had successfully overcome comparable obstacles and found meaningful careers with young people who were in danger. Professionals from a range of industries, including business, the arts, and public service, gave their time as mentors to the young people, offering them advice, encouragement, and listening. The program gave the young participants a safe place to talk about their goals, anxieties, and challenges by offering them emotional support, career assistance, and scheduled activities. Many participants' lives were impacted as these interactions developed into true bonds of respect and trust over time. Success stories from the program started to surface: kids who had been on the verge of abandoning were suddenly graduating, while other kids were starting college or getting their first jobs.

6. Bridge of Books

In a divided community where language barriers had created significant gaps between immigrant and native populations, a local library initiated a "Bridge of Books" program. The program involved bilingual storytelling sessions and the distribution of books in multiple languages. It aimed to foster understanding and connection among the community's diverse groups, particularly focusing on children.

The library became a communal hub where families from different backgrounds gathered, children played and learned together, and parents exchanged stories and experiences. This program not only promoted literacy but also served as a bridge, uniting the community through the shared joy of storytelling and the universal appeal of narratives.

Thus, these stories show the power of compassion to heal spirits and bridge gaps. Every story reminds us that kindness and empathy are powerful forces that can unite people, mend old wounds, and build a more cohesive and encouraging society.

Communities may turn conflicts into chances for development and togetherness by understanding and caring for one another, demonstrating the strength found in compassionate acts.

The Value of True Connections in Spiritual Growth

In the journey of personal and spiritual development, the creation and nurturing of genuine relationships are not just beneficial; they are essential. Let's explore how deeply our spiritual well-being is intertwined with the communities we build and the authentic bonds we foster.

1.   The Foundation of Community

Community forms the foundation of spiritual growth by facilitating connections beyond one self, anchoring spirituality in the interactions and relationships we foster. By engaging with others, individuals gain unique insights and reflections that are crucial for deepening their understanding of themselves and the broader spiritual truths. These connections provide spiritual principles like empathy and compassion, which are real-world examples, enabling people to embody these ideals in their daily lives.

A community also provides a secure environment for spiritual exploration and belief expression, fostering personal development through mutual support and shared experiences. This collaborative environment not only enriches individual lives but also solidifies collective spiritual resilience, promoting a unified pursuit of higher truths and shared goals.

2.   The Role of Authenticity in Relationships

Authenticity is essential in nurturing profound spiritual connections. By being genuine, individuals create a trustworthy environment where members feel safe to share their spiritual struggles and victories.

This honesty paves the way for meaningful relationships that are characterized by deep understanding and mutual respect. Such environments foster not only individual growth but also communal resilience, as members support each other in navigating the challenges of spiritual paths. Authentic relationships thus form a crucial framework within which individuals can explore and affirm their spiritual identities and practices. They enable transparency that dissolves barriers and fosters a deeper engagement with spiritual teachings and communal activities.

3.   Learning from Collective Wisdom

Communities rich in honesty and openness become invaluable sources of collective wisdom, facilitating growth and learning for all members. As individuals share their personal experiences, the entire community gains insights and lessons that contribute to a collective pool of knowledge.

This process is particularly powerful in settings that involve communal worship or meditation, where the shared spiritual energy enhances personal experiences and deepens connections.

Engaging with this collective wisdom allows members to draw strength and guidance, enriching their spiritual journeys and fostering a culture of continuous learning and support. This collaborative learning environment is a testament to the community's power to elevate individual experiences into collective insights.

4. The Support System

The support provided by a spiritual community is crucial, especially when navigating the challenging aspects of spiritual growth. Such a network offers not just emotional support but also practical advice and companionship. When individuals share hardships and rejoice in one other's victories, these connections help to lessen the isolation and increase the manageability of the spiritual path.

As a result, the group becomes an invaluable resource for support and motivation, enabling every individual to continue and grow on their spiritual journey and guaranteeing that no one has to face challenges on their own. Members' deep sense of commitment and belonging is fostered by this shared journey, which strengthens their devotion to spiritual development.

5. Fostering Empathy and Compassion

In a community where people share their spiritual and personal journeys, empathy and compassion naturally flourish. Since everyone is vulnerable with one another, this fosters compassion, fortifying social ties and bringing these fundamental spiritual principles into everyday existence. In addition to encouraging personal development, such an atmosphere fosters a sense of understanding and concern among all community members, enlightening it as a center of compassion and empathy. This enhances the person's spiritual practice and brings these virtues into wider social interactions. It catalyzes a ripple effect, where spiritual teachings transform personal interactions, thus affecting broader community and societal norms.

6.   Catalyzing Personal Transformation

The community serves as a dynamic catalyst for personal transformation, providing motivation and accountability that can spur individuals to engage more deeply with their spiritual practices. Community members are encouraged to study and take up spiritual practices that may seem intimidating on their own because of their shared passion and dedication. Because members are inspired to step outside of their comfort zones and adopt novel spiritual practices and insights, this collective energy frequently results in remarkable personal transformations. In addition to quickening the process of personal evolution, such a nurturing atmosphere also fosters a thriving spiritual ecosystem that supports ongoing development and transformation.

7.   Sustaining Spiritual Practice

Regular interaction and shared activities within a community play a crucial role in sustaining members' spiritual practices. Consistent spiritual practice is vital for long-term growth, and organizing group meditations, discussions, and prayer sessions can help maintain this practice. This routine not only helps individuals to stay focused on their spiritual objectives but also reinforces their commitment to their path. The community, therefore, acts as a reinforcing mechanism that supports the spiritual discipline and growth of its members, making it easier for them to maintain their spiritual momentum. Regular gatherings also foster a collective identity and spirit, which reinforces the community's role in each member's spiritual life.

In essence, spiritual growth is greatly enhanced by genuine connections and a supportive community. These relationships provide a foundation for deeper understanding, a platform for shared learning, and a network of support that spans all emotional landscapes.

As individuals come together in their quest for spiritual enlightenment, they build a collective strength that amplifies their own personal growth. Through this communal engagement, the path toward spiritual fulfillment becomes a shared venture characterized by joint discoveries and mutual triumphs. This collective journey not only deepens individual practices but also strengthens the community's unity and purpose, creating a sustainable spiritual legacy.

Chapter 6: Living Your Truth - The Courage to be Seen

"To thine own self be true, and it must follow, as the night the day, thou canst not then be false to any man."

-William Shakespeare.

This profound advice captures the essence of living authentically, asserting that being true to oneself is both a spiritual practice and a bold statement of authenticity. When individuals embrace their genuine selves, they unlock a deeper connection with their core values and beliefs, facilitating a pathway that is both personally fulfilling and spiritually enriching.

This frees them from the constraints of societal norms, enabling a more truthful and dynamic display of their individuality. Moreover, by following this route, people are better prepared to manage life's obstacles, nurturing resilience and a sense of internal calm that pervades their daily experiences.

Authenticity in spiritual realms is often portrayed as a life in tune with one's deepest truths. Across various spiritual traditions, there is a pronounced focus on the importance of self-awareness and self-acceptance as crucial elements for personal development and enlightenment.

This spiritual path toward authenticity is essentially about removing the layers of social expectations and personal doubts to reveal a core unaffected by external factors. Rediscovering the essence of one's actual self requires facing deeply rooted ideas and behaviors, which may be a challenging yet rewarding process. Along the way, every step strengthens the basis for long-lasting spiritual and emotional well-being in addition to providing a moment of clarity.

Individuals who follow this route progressively remove the masks and person as they unintentionally took on as a result of cultural and familial upbringing. This process of removing layers is not just metaphorical; it also entails tangible exercises like writing, meditation, and thoughtful reflection, which reduce outside distractions and promote introspection.

By investigating the origins of their ideas and feelings, people can investigate the nuances of their identities through these practices, which frequently results in important insights into their goals and moral principles. Consequently, these revelations enable individuals to make more thoughtful and informed decisions, bringing their behaviors closer to their own truths.

This journey strengthens one's connection with the divine or with universal principles, supporting the idea that one's own truth serves as a doorway to a deeper spiritual understanding. The realization of a higher, more universal self is often equated with the finding of one's true self in several spiritual frameworks, including Hinduism and Sufism.

Authenticity in these traditions involves realizing one's place and connection in a greater cosmic order, in addition to self-knowledge. For instance, the concept of "Atman," the true self, which is believed to be the same as "Brahman," the universal spirit, is frequently used in Hindu philosophy to convey this. Living authentically leads to the realization of this identity, which offers an escape from the cycle of rebirth and sorrow. This profound realization is a great source of motivation for those who are seeking a better understanding of themselves and spiritual liberation. In practical terms, a more heartfelt and sincere engagement with the outside world results from the authenticity acquired from spiritual practice. People make decisions and behave in ways that increasingly mirror their inner values and beliefs as they move closer to their actual selves.

Their relationships with others are impacted by this alignment, which fosters relationships built on sincere understanding and respect. It also enhances their personal life. Living authentically and spiritually promotes honesty and integrity, leading to a positive impact on society through communal living and group decision-making. This wider effect promotes an honest and transparent culture, which is essential for the well-being of individuals as well as communities.

Living a life that is authentic to oneself and establishing a strong connection with one's inner spirit are key components of the spiritual dimension of authenticity. Because there is less tension between one's inner principles and external acts, such a lifestyle encourages inner serenity and joy.

Spirituality often teaches that this alignment is not just beneficial but essential for reaching higher states of consciousness and fulfillment.

One enters a transforming path by committing to this real existence, which not only calms the soul but also fortifies one's spiritual resilience. Thus, pursuing authenticity serves as a means of reaching higher levels of fulfillment and spiritual enlightenment. In a societal context, living authentically is a courageous act because it defies conventions and expectations that frequently prescribe what people should feel, think, and do. People who choose authenticity over societal approval are making a strong statement about how important personal integrity is.

Others may be motivated to reevaluate their own decisions and how much their lives actually reflect who they really are as a result of this. Additionally, by preventing cultural stagnation, this act of authenticity can promote a community that is more vibrant and forward-thinking. People who show such bravery not only uphold their own moral principles but also open the door for more significant societal changes and advancements.

Take, for example, the case of Malala Yousafzai, a Pakistani lady who championed the cause of girls' education in a region where such a position was both rare and perilous. Her determination to live a true life and voice her opinions in the face of serious social consequences—including a potentially fatal attack—emphasized her preference for authenticity over conformity.

Malala's actions confronted social conventions and ignited worldwide discussions on education and women's rights, motivating others globally to advocate for their convictions and rights. Her bravery not only transformed her personal trajectory but also shaped the international dialogue on gender fairness and the right to education, establishing her as a worldwide icon of defiance against suppression. Similarly, in the business realm, Shantanu Narayen, CEO of Adobe Systems, is recognized for his dedication to authenticity. Under his direction, Adobe has highlighted openness and staff well-being, shifting from conventional business methods such as yearly performance evaluations to a more ongoing and transparent feedback mechanism.

This approach has increased staff retention and happiness while spurring innovation and growth, demonstrating that authenticity can positively impact corporate outcomes. Narayen has contributed to the development of an innovative workplace that not only helps its employees in significant ways but also thrives on honesty and personal growth·

Another inspiring example is Satya Nadella, CEO of Microsoft, who has been instrumental in transforming the company's culture since taking the helm in 2014. Under Nadella's leadership, Microsoft shifted from a competitive and harsh environment to one focused on growth, learning, and empathy.

Nadella's belief in "hitting refresh" on perspectives and behaviors that are no longer beneficial to the business or its staff served as the foundation for this cultural revolution Nadella advocates for an empathetic work environment that promotes employee happiness, engagement, innovation, and growth opportunities. His dedication to leadership that is genuine and empathetic demonstrates how these qualities may have a big impact on company culture and result in notable financial gains.

These examples show how choosing to live authentically can serve as a powerful catalyst for change, challenging outdated norms and inspiring others to live more genuinely. As individuals like Malala, leaders like Narayen, and visionaries like Satya Nadella demonstrate their true selves, they achieve personal fulfillment and encourage a broader cultural shift toward more openness and integrity in various societal spheres. Their actions serve as a reminder that authentic living can drive profound societal change, pushing boundaries and setting new precedents for future generations.

Authentic living serves as a beacon for others, offering an alternative way of living that emphasizes genuine self-expression over conformity. It encourages a society where diversity of thought and being is truly valued, creating a more vibrant and dynamic community. Each person who chooses this path helps to construct a cultural fabric that is richer and more accepting of individual differences. *"As iron sharpens iron, so one person sharpens another·"* This proverb highlights how authentic interactions not only refine our own character but also enhance those around us, fostering a community that thrives on mutual improvement and understanding.

Such an environment nurtures individual growth and bolsters societal evolution, making authenticity a vital element of cultural advancement. This influence goes beyond mere personal benefit, catalyzing a collective shift that enriches community values and social interactions.

Authenticity enriches relationships by cultivating trust and openness. When people are truthful to themselves, they are more inclined to partake in sincere and open communication, laying the foundation for deeper and more impactful connections. In a community environment, authenticity encourages a culture of clarity and honest interaction, which can foster stronger and more unified social ties. This foundation of truthfulness enables a more profound and impactful collaboration among community members. By strengthening these bonds, authenticity paves the way for a more connected and responsive community. Moreover, there is a stronger sense of acceptance and belonging in a group where authenticity is valued. Individuals feel appreciated for who they are rather than just what they fit into. People feel comfortable expressing who they are in a supportive environment created by this acceptance, which further improves individual and societal well-being.

Because these communities are based on a strong foundation of respect and understanding for one another, they are better suited to overcome obstacles as a group. As Brené Brown wisely said, *'Authenticity is the daily practice of letting go of who we think we're supposed to be and embracing who we are.'* This principle is critical in creating a nurturing and inclusive society.

Being true to oneself as a spiritual practice and a bold statement of authenticity is a powerful approach to living. It boosts personal fulfillment and spiritual development and deeply influences relationships and community interactions. Despite external pressures and expectations, accepting one's genuine self is proof of personal strength and a commitment to a life of genuineness.

Through this practice, individuals achieve deeper self-comprehension and peace and foster a more inclusive, accepting, and dynamic society.

Authenticity has the capacity to transform not just the individual but also the community, promoting an appreciation and celebration of the distinctive contributions made by each member of the individual.

Practical Exercises for Aligning Daily Actions with Personal Values

"The only way to do great work is to love what you do"

-Steve Jobs.

Aligning our daily actions with our core principles and truths is an intellectual ideal and a vital necessity for a fulfilling life.

This harmony ensures that each choice and behavior moves us toward our objectives and deeply aligns with our moral integrity and principles. Here are practical exercises designed to help people consistently embody their core values and truths in their day-to-day actions.

Exercise 1: Values Clarification

Understanding and determining what is truly significant to you is fundamental to living authentically. Prior to harmonizing one's actions with values, it is imperative to ascertain the nature of those values.

Assign a list of personal values that hold significance to you, including but not limited to honesty, compassion, innovation, and resilience.

Once you have compiled a comprehensive list of these values, arrange them in order of importance to your sense of self. Identifying these values is the initial step in cultivating a life of greater purpose and congruence by ensuring that each decision you make is consistent with your personal stance.

Steps:

1. List out values that resonate with you.

2. Prioritize them from most to least important.

3. Choose the top five values that are most important to you.

4. For each value, write a brief statement that explains why it is significant to you.

This exercise helps you make decisions that are in harmony with your personal ethos, making your actions more authentic and intentional.

Exercise 2: Daily Reflection

Incorporating contemplation into your daily routine can significantly enhance your self-awareness and capacity to act in accordance with your principles. Reflection is an effective strategy for personal growth and can help ensure that your daily behaviors mirror your principles.

Allocate a few minutes each day to contemplate your behaviors and decisions.

The question is whether these behaviors align with your principles and how you might modify them to better reflect your truths. This process fosters a deeper connection with your personal ethos and challenges you to continual self-improvement.

Steps:

1. At the end of each day, jot down key actions and decisions you made.

2. Assess whether these actions aligned with your top values.

3. Consider what you could improve to enhance alignment with your values.

4. Plan specific actions for the next day to reflect your values better.

Regular reflection not only helps in reinforcing values but also promotes a mindful approach to everyday living.

Exercise 3: Setting Intentions

Starting each day with a clear focus can transform how you navigate your daily life. Set clear intentions each morning that align with your values. This practice makes living by abstract values throughout the day when they are turned into tangible plans simpler. You can live a more purposeful and focused life by actively stating your intentions, increasing the likelihood that your daily actions will be consistent with your core values.

Steps:

1. Write down three intentions for the day that align with your values each morning.

2. Keep these intentions visible throughout the day.

3. Review these intentions at the end of the day to evaluate your adherence to them.

Setting intentions helps to focus your day on what truly matters to you, acting as a guide for your actions.

Exercise 4: Accountability Partners

The journey to living authentically doesn't have to be a solitary one. Sharing your goals and values with a trusted friend or colleague can help maintain your commitment to living authentically. An accountability partner can provide support, offer constructive feedback, and help you stay focused on aligning your actions with your values. This relationship encourages continuous reflection and growth, reinforcing your dedication to your values through mutual support and regular engagement.

Steps:

1. Choose a trusted individual who understands and respects your values.

2. Regularly share your goals and daily intentions with them.

3. Meet or talk regularly to discuss progress and challenges.

4. Offer mutual support and encouragement to adhere to each other's values.

This mutual engagement fosters a supportive environment for personal growth and authenticity.

Exercise 5: Value-Based Decision-Making

Decisions shape our lives, and syncing them with our fundamental values is essential for authentic living. Employ your established values as a compass when confronted with choices, regardless of their scale. This could involve devising a straight forward diagram or checklist that positions your values at the heart of your decision-making process. By persistently aligning your choices with your values, you cultivate a life that is goal-oriented and mirrors your true essence in daily situations.

Steps:

1. Define the decision to be made.

2. List possible options or actions.

3. Evaluate each option against your top values.

4. Choose the option that best aligns with these values.

Using values as a decision-making filter ensures that one's actions consistently align with one's deepest truths, even in challenging situations.

Exercise 6: Mindful Consumption

This exercise involves heightening awareness of your consumption patterns—whether it pertains to purchasing items, engaging with media, or participating in activities—and ensuring they align with your principles. By intentionally opting for choices that reflect your values, you manage the influence you exert on yourself and your surroundings. This conscious choice fosters a lifestyle that is not only driven by values but also sustainable and accountable.

Steps:

1. Consider how it aligns with your values before purchasing or consuming media.

2. Ask yourself if this choice supports what you stand for.

3. Opt for alternatives that better reflect your values when necessary.

Mindful consumption helps people live more authentically and promotes sustainability and responsibility.

Exercise 7: Visual Reminders

Visual cues can be powerful motivators and reminders of our deepest values. This exercise involves creating visual reminders that can help keep your values front and center in your daily life. Placing these reminders in strategic locations helps to constantly nudge you toward behaviors consistent with your values, thereby enhancing your daily living with reminders of who you aspire to be.

Steps:

1. Create small visual reminders like posters, wallpapers, or objects that represent your values.

2. Place them in your workspace, home, or digital devices.

3. Use these visuals as cues to guide your behavior throughout the day.

Visual reminders are constant prompts to act in ways consistent with your deepest values and truths.

Exercise 8: Community Engagement

Actively participating in community activities that reflect your values can reinforce your commitment. This exercise involves engaging with groups or initiatives that align with your personal truths.

By connecting with others who share your values, you not only enrich your own life but also contribute to the vitality of your community. This active participation is a robust way to live out your values visibly and impactfully.

Steps:

1. Identify community projects or groups that resonate with your values.

2. Participate in activities or volunteer your time.

3. Use these opportunities to connect with others who share your values.

Community engagement enhances your sense of connection and commitment to your values, enriching both your personal life and your wider community.

Regular exercises can transform simple tasks into habitual actions that align your daily life with your deepest values and truths. By embedding these values into your daily actions, you foster a life of authenticity and fulfillment rooted deeply in what truly matters to you.

This commitment enhances personal integrity and profoundly influences one's interactions and relationships, creating a ripple effect that extends beyond the individual to the wider community.

Inspiring Examples of Courage and Integrity in Action

Throughout history and contemporary times, numerous individuals have stood out as beacons of authenticity, fearlessly living their truths and inspiring others to embrace their own. This account explores the lives and impacts of such individuals, demonstrating how authenticity can lead to significant societal change and personal fulfillment.

1. Rosa Parks: A Quiet Strength

Rosa Parks is revered for her quiet, dignified insistence on living an authentic life and her significant contribution to the Civil Rights Movement. Her very honest refusal to give up her seat to a white passenger on December 1, 1955, in Montgomery, Alabama, aroused widespread protest and finally resulted in a significant legislative change.

By taking a silent stand, Parks showed the effectiveness of resistance and encouraged many others to ask themselves, "What can my truthful living achieve?" Her legacy serves as a constant reminder that sincere deeds, no matter how modest at first, have the power to spark enormous transformations and confront systemic injustices. The life of Rosa Parks is a moving example of how brave individual actions can spur a community's advancement toward more justice and equality.

2.   Chimamanda Ngozi Adichie: Amplifying Voices and Stories

Chimamanda Ngozi Adichie, a Nigerian author and renowned speaker, has garnered global acclaim for her powerful storytelling and insightful commentary on race, identity, and feminism. Her novels, such as "Half of a Yellow Sun," "Americanah," and "Purple Hibiscus," delve into the complexities of Nigerian society and the African diaspora, offering readers a nuanced understanding of diverse experiences. Adichie's TED Talk, "We Should All Be Feminists," has further amplified her voice, influencing discussions on gender equality worldwide. Through her writing and public speaking, Adichie challenges stereotypes and advocates for authentic representation in literature and media.

Her work inspires others to embrace their identities and share their stories, highlighting the transformative power of literature in fostering empathy and understanding. Adichie's commitment to truth and authenticity in her narratives encourages a deeper appreciation of cultural diversity and social justice, making her a leading figure in contemporary literature and activism.

3.   Jane Goodall: Pioneering Conservation and Environmental Advocacy

Jane Goodall, a globally acclaimed primatologist and environmental advocate, has utilized her detailed observations of chimpanzee behavior to promote ecological protection and animal welfare. Through her pioneering research at Gombe Stream National Park in Tanzania, Goodall was the pioneer in noting chimpanzees creating and utilizing tools, an activity once thought unique to humans. Her discoveries have contested established scientific beliefs and transformed our comprehension of the natural environment. Beyond her fieldwork, Goodall's commitment led to the establishment of the Jane Goodall Institute, which advocates for ecological sustainability and worldwide wildlife protection. Her tireless work and authentic bond with nature have motivated many to advocate for environmental care, demonstrating that a life lived with passion and genuineness can significantly alter ecological conservation and responsibility perspectives.

4. Keanu Reeves: Humility and Simplicity

In addition to his acting skills, Hollywood actor Keanu Reeves is renowned for his modest way of living and deep humility. Despite his fame and success, Reeves is frequently seen taking public transit, being polite to his followers, and discreetly contributing to humanitarian causes. His sincerity in an industry often noted for its superficiality motivates others to appreciate simplicity and kindness rather than material achievement. Keanu exemplifies a challenge to the standard Hollywood story and prompts others to rethink their choices and priorities by opting to lead a simple life and concentrate on essential values. His way of life underscores authenticity and compassion, which can thrive even in settings typically characterized by materialism and self-interest.

5. Greta Thunberg: A Young Activist's Voice

Swedish environmental activist Greta Thunberg began her journey to global influence by protesting outside the Swedish parliament when she was 15. Her straightforward, factual approach to climate change has mobilized a new generation of activists and significantly impacted global discourse on environmental policies. Greta's example demonstrates that, regardless of age, leading an authentic life and being devoted to one's principles may effect change. Many young people are still motivated to take action for their future by her unwavering activism and refusal to be silenced, highlighting the importance of genuine voices in igniting global dialogues. Greta exemplifies how passion and persistence in advocacy can draw attention to critical global issues and inspire action at all levels of society.

6. Tim Cook: Leading with Pride

Tim Cook, the CEO of Apple Inc., has used his position to promote human rights, environmental responsibility, and privacy. Being among the first openly gay CEOs of a large company, he has advocated for diversity and inclusivity in the IT sector and beyond using his platform. His leadership encourages other executives and businesses to prioritize ethical standards since it demonstrates his dedication to honesty in both his personal identity and company obligations. Cook establishes an example for other corporate executives to follow by showing how influential positions may be used to promote diversity and support underrepresented groups. His strategy demonstrates how genuine leadership at the highest level can persuade a whole sector to embrace more forward-thinking and inclusive procedures. These individuals are good examples of the impact of leading an authentic life. They show that people may inspire change, promote acceptance, and spearhead movements when they choose to live out their truths in the face of fear or rejection.

Their experiences are compelling reminders that authenticity is a social force that may affect large-scale change in addition to being a personal virtue.

These leaders inspire us to consider how our true selves can improve the world by accepting who they are. Their legacies teach us that when we live by who we really are, we inspire others to follow suit, bringing about positive change that spreads throughout generations and societies.

Chapter 7: From Veil to Valor - Embracing the Journey Ahead

As mentioned throughout the book, the journey from harboring self-doubt to achieving spiritual awareness and living genuinely is a dynamic process, less about dramatic revelations and more about gradual acceptance and understanding of one's inner self. This path starts in a place familiar to many: self-doubt. Individuals may question their abilities, worth, or decisions, often triggered by life's various challenges, such as career changes, relationship issues, or significant personal setbacks. Recognizing these moments as opportunities for growth rather than signs of failure is crucial to moving forward. This initial phase sets the groundwork for a transformative personal journey that unfolds over time. Overcoming these doubts requires a proactive approach to self-examination and the willingness to face uncomfortable truths.

To progress, individuals engage with their internal dialogue, actively listening to and reflecting on the inner voices that often create doubt. Through practices like meditation, reflective writing, or therapy, it becomes possible to distinguish between irrational fears and realistic assessments.

This phase of the journey is critical as it allows individuals to challenge their limiting beliefs and gradually replace them with supportive and constructive thoughts. Overcoming these mental barriers opens the door to new possibilities, fostering a stronger sense of self and a more focused direction in life. It is a transformative process that builds the foundation for a renewed perception of self-worth and capabilities. As one continues to challenge personal doubts, various experiences along the way contribute to learning and growth. These include successes and failures, each carrying valuable lessons about resilience, adaptability, and perseverance.

Such experiences are instrumental in teaching how to navigate future challenges with increased confidence and insight. They also help people develop the courage to take risks and the insight to learn from every failure, which improves their capacity to deal with life's challenges.

As individuals gain insight from these experiences, they progressively attain a more profound state of spiritual consciousness. Experiencing this state of awareness goes beyond what's associated with religion or culture, exploring the core essence of being fully aware and aligned with one's own beliefs, goals, and dreams. Engaging in activities that unite the mind and body, like yoga, plays a key role in promoting this by encouraging individuals to slow down, focus on the moment, and develop a deeper understanding of themselves and their surroundings.

The endpoint of this journey is achieving authenticity; it calls for integrating one's actions with one's true self and core values. Living authentically does not mean striving for perfection but rather holding onto honesty and integrity in all dealings with oneself and others.

It signifies a commitment to one's well-being and joy, rooted in a solid grasp of what brings happiness and significance to one's existence. By continuously matching actions with personal principles, individuals enrich their own lives and positively impact those around them, generating a wave of authenticity and satisfaction. This ultimate stage is marked by the conscious decision to live by one's values and to cultivate sincere relationships with others. To achieve true personal growth, it's important to acknowledge that this path is not straight but cyclic, involving continual cycles of doubt, reaffirmation, education, and unlearning. It demands persistent contemplation and modification as one's comprehension of oneself deepens over time.

Although this path is arduous, it is vital for anyone aspiring to lead a fulfilled and meaningful life, showing the resilience of the human spirit and its ability for growth and change. Each advance in this cycle brings a revitalized commitment and energy, reinforcing the continuous nature of personal and spiritual development. Through constant self-exploration and adjustment, individuals endlessly improve their life's narrative, securing continuous personal evolution and satisfaction.

Reaffirming the Endless Adventure of Personal Growth

Building on the above foundation, pursuing personal growth and self-discovery is a nonstop journey that requires commitment, patience, and resilience. It is an adventure that never truly ends, offering new opportunities for learning and development at every stage of life.

Embracing this journey means understanding that growth is a perpetual process, not a destination. Each step forward brings renewed commitment and energy, reinforcing the continuous nature of personal development. A key element of personal growth is engaging in introspection. This includes scrutinizing one's thoughts, deeds, and experiences. Introspection helps individuals identify areas for improvement and acknowledge their successes. In "Atomic Habits" by James Clear, the emphasis is placed on adopting minor adjustments to yield substantial outcomes. Through consistent self-assessment and practicing small, beneficial habits, one can make choices corresponding to their values and objectives.

Additionally, introspection enhances comprehension of personal drives, allowing individuals to tackle the fundamental reasons for their actions. This practice also promotes a growth mentality, aiding individuals in seeing obstacles as opportunities for learning.

Establishing objectives is a potent method to remain dedicated to personal advancement. Goals offer direction and intent, aiding individuals in concentrating their efforts on essential matters. It's crucial to set both short-term and long-term goals that are feasible and achievable. As Stephen Covey describes in "The 7 Habits of Highly Effective People," fulfilling these goals, regardless of their size, imparts a sense of achievement and fuels further advancement. The path of self-exploration also encompasses acquiring knowledge and new experiences. Continuous education is vital for individual growth, attainable through formal schooling, reading, travel, or taking up new hobbies. Each new insight or experience expands our viewpoints and furnishes us with the tools to manage different life aspects.

Building and maintaining healthy relationships is a crucial component of personal growth. Engaging with others opens up avenues to absorb varied viewpoints and acquire an understanding of our actions. Beneficial connections provide backing, motivation, and helpful critiques, all fundamental for individual development. In "How to Win Friends and Influence People," Dale Carnegie stresses the significance of beneficial exchanges for individual achievement. Being surrounded by positive forces can influence one's development trajectory.

The individual enhancement also entails developing self-insight. Comprehending one's strengths, limitations, values, and convictions is vital for informed choice-making and setting substantial objectives. Self-insight enables individuals to live genuinely and synchronize their behaviors with their authentic selves, fostering self-acceptance and assurance.

Resilience is a key quality that bolsters individual development. The path to advancement is not always linear; it frequently encounters setbacks and hurdles. Cultivating resilience involves mastering these challenges and perceiving them as avenues for growth. As Viktor Frankl outlines in "Man's Search for Meaning," resilience cultivates a hopeful attitude, inspiring individuals to persist forward despite hardships. Mindfulness is also a crucial practice that supports individual growth. Being mindful entails staying present and fully engaging with one's experiences. Mindfulness boosts self-insight and aids individuals in managing stress and emotions effectively. Techniques such as meditation and deep breathing can enhance mindfulness, contributing to overall health and growth.

Self-care forms an essential element of personal development. Taking care of physical, mental, and emotional well-being is essential as these factors sustain the energy required for growth throughout life. Self-care practices vary from person to person but may include regular exercise, healthy eating, adequate rest, and engaging in activities that bring joy and relaxation. Brené Brown, in "The Gifts of Imperfection," discusses how embracing vulnerability can lead to personal growth. To be vulnerable is to be receptive to new experiences and prepared to take chances. Courage and honesty that come from vulnerability help people to move outside of their comfort zones. Deeper connections to oneself and others are encouraged, which advances emotional and personal growth.

A further component of developing personally is gratitude. Being grateful is seeing and enjoying the good things in life. In "The Gratitude Diaries," Janice Kaplan shows how thankfulness helps one to focus on what is abundant rather than what is lacking, therefore promoting a happy outlook. It improves general health and fosters a more upbeat perspective on life, which promotes ongoing development. Personal growth requires perseverance and the virtue of tolerance. Growth occurs gradually over time. Consistent effort and dedication are required. Patience enables individuals to maintain their dedication to their endeavors, notwithstanding the apparent slowness of their progress. Perseverance ensures that they continue moving forward despite setbacks and challenges.

Reflecting on past experiences is a valuable tool for personal growth. By examining past actions and outcomes, individuals can learn important lessons and apply them to future decisions. In "Educated," the author Tara Westover reflects on her life to make sense of her experiences and foster growth. Reflection promotes self-awareness and helps individuals identify patterns in their behavior, enabling them to make positive changes. Personal growth is an individual journey, and each person's path is unique. It is important to recognize that there is no one-size-fits-all approach to self-discovery. What works for one person may not work for another. Embracing one's individuality and finding what resonates personally is key to a successful growth journey.

It is beneficial for one's growth to reflect on prior experiences. Through critical analysis of previous actions and their corresponding results, individuals can acquire valuable insights that can be implemented in subsequent decision-making processes. Tara Westover, the author of "Educated," attempts to make meaning of her life's experiences and promotes personal development through introspection. Reflection fosters self-awareness and facilitates the recognition of behavioral patterns, empowering individuals to enact constructive transformations. Every person's route to personal growth is different, and it is an individual journey. It's critical to understand that there isn't a single, universal strategy for self-discovery.

Another important aspect of personal growth is setting boundaries. Boundaries safeguard one's health and ensure needs are met. Setting boundaries involves recognizing limits and articulating them effectively. The book "Boundaries: When to Say Yes, How to Say No to Take Control of Your Life" by Drs. Henry Cloud and John Townsend discusses healthy boundaries fostering self-esteem and helping maintain relationships, which are essentials for progression.

Seeking evaluations from others can also bolster growth. Constructive feedback yields a valuable understanding of conduct and performance. It identifies regions for enhancement and reiterates positives. Being receptive to feedback demonstrates readiness to evolve and advance, cultivating continual evolution. Personal growth is not only about individual benefits, but it also contributes to the well-being of others. Acts of compassion and empathy enhance development by fostering connection and reinforcing purpose. The authors of "The Book of Joy" highlight that helping others provides fulfillment and gives meaning to values. Additionally, giving back creates positive ripples that can inspire similar generosity in others. This collective effort strengthens communities while enriching each individual's journey.

Thus, the journey of growth and discovery demands commitment, patience, and resilience to change. It involves such key attributes as introspection, embracing change, goal-setting, seeking knowledge, building relationships, cultivating self-awareness, developing tolerance, mindfulness, self-care, vulnerability, gratitude, patience, perseverance, experience reflection, identity recognition, boundaries, feedback, and aiding others.

Each element crucially supports continuous self-evolution. Remaining dedicated to this endless expedition allows living purposefully and to one's full potential, demonstrating boundless opportunity for transformation.

This cyclical nature of growth is exemplified in Elara's journey from self-doubt to spiritual awareness. Elara's transformation commenced amidst a period of adversity in her life. Following years of excessive work as a freelance writer that led to exhaustion, she began to doubt her value and capabilities. During the early stages of her transformation, she engaged in a profound process of introspection. By documenting her thoughts and emotions in a journal, she was able to confront and gain insight into her uncertainties. Elara also initiated the practice of meditation, an activity that facilitated her ability to discern irrational anxieties from rational concerns. By engaging in these routines, she progressively substituted pessimistic thoughts for constructive and encouraging ones, thereby establishing the foundation for her own development.

By adopting a proactive stance toward self-examination, she surmounted her mental obstacles and cultivated a more robust self-perception and a more lucid life trajectory.

She continued her journey and encountered a variety of circumstances that contributed to her development and growth. By becoming a member of a local hiking group, she not only enhanced her physical health but also fostered a stronger bond with both nature and herself.

By enduring the rigors and successes of trekking challenging trails, she gained invaluable insight into the virtues of perseverance and flexibility. She gained confidence from these experiences and learned to bravely confront new obstacles.

Over time, Elara developed an elevated state of spiritual consciousness distinguished by a profound congruence with her personal principles and an unmistakable intention.

Since attaining this new consciousness, she consistently conducted herself more authentically, reflecting her true self. Through her actions, she enhanced her personal life and positively influenced those in her vicinity, cultivating authentic relationships and a heightened sense of satisfaction.

The Profound Impact of Authentic Living

Living authentically — aligning one's actions with one's true self—is a journey that benefits the individual and the broader world. As the proverb goes, *"To thine own self be true,"* this timeless advice underlines the significance of authenticity as a foundation for personal and communal well-being.

Individual Impact of Living Authentically

When individuals commit to understanding and expressing their genuine selves, they experience a heightened sense of fulfillment. This self-realization fosters an environment where one's decisions and actions are guided by personal values and beliefs rather than societal expectations. The result is a life with less regret and more satisfaction, as decisions are made with confidence and integrity. This alignment leads to a more resilient and adaptable personality because when challenges arise, those who are grounded in their true selves can navigate difficulties with greater ease and less internal conflict. *"A bird does not sing because it has an answer. It sings because it has a song,"* this Chinese proverb captures the essence of living authentically and expressing oneself freely and naturally.

Moreover, living authentically encourages emotional well-being. By honoring their emotions and thoughts, individuals cultivate a healthier mental state. This is because suppressing one's true feelings or modifying behaviors to fit external standards often leads to stress and anxiety. Conversely, authenticity allows for a more open and honest relationship with oneself, enhancing mental clarity and emotional stability.

Community Impact of Authentic Living

The benefits of living authentically extend beyond the individual, influencing the community. When people interact with someone genuine and transparent, they are often inspired to express their authenticity. This creates a culture of honesty and trust within communities, where members feel safer to share their true selves without fear of judgment. Such environments foster deeper, more meaningful relationships crucial for community solidarity and support. This ripple effect of authenticity enhances communal resilience and adaptability, allowing people to support each other through challenges and transitions more effectively. Moreover, it promotes an atmosphere of mutual respect and understanding, enriching the social fabric of the community.

Authentic individuals often embody a sense of purpose that motivates them to contribute positively to their surroundings. They tend to engage in activities and roles that reflect their values and passions, leading to personal fulfillment and driving community progress.

Their genuine enthusiasm and commitment can inspire others and catalyze collective action toward shared goals. *"It takes a village to raise a child"* shows how collective authenticity can empower communities. By living authentically, individuals contribute to a proactive engagement and collaboration culture, making it easier for communities to initiate and sustain change. This dynamic involvement in community life uplifts individual participants and strengthens the collective capacity for achieving common objectives. In the realm of leadership, authentic leaders are particularly impactful. They lead by example, showing that one can succeed while upholding one's principles. These leaders build trust and earn respect through consistent and transparent actions, creating a positive work environment and fostering a culture of integrity. Teams guided by authentic leaders are typically more engaged, motivated, and productive, which can translate into broader societal benefits. This leadership style also helps attract and retain talent who value transparency and ethics, further enhancing organizational stability and reputation. Moreover, such leaders inspire others to adopt similar behaviors, fostering a cycle of authenticity permeating various levels of interactions and decision-making processes.

Global Impact of Authenticity

On a global scale, authenticity can drive societal progress by promoting more ethical behaviors and practices. As more individuals and leaders commit to authenticity, they set standards prioritizing ethics over profit or personal gain. This shift can significantly change how businesses operate, influencing them to adopt more sustainable and fair practices.

Consequently, this could help address some of the world's critical challenges, such as environmental degradation, inequality, and corruption. This transformation toward ethical practices also supports the long-term viability of businesses, creating a foundation for sustained economic growth that does not sacrifice social or environmental well-being.

Additionally, societies embracing authenticity pave the way for policies that safeguard human rights and promote equality, making ethical behavior a hallmark of modern governance and corporate strategy. Authenticity also plays a crucial role in cultural exchange and global understanding. When individuals from different backgrounds share their true selves, it fosters a greater appreciation for diversity and encourages a deeper understanding of various cultural perspectives. This can reduce prejudices and misunderstandings, promoting a more inclusive and harmonious global community. Through such exchanges, people discover the underlying similarities that unite us across cultural divides, enhancing global solidarity.

Furthermore, this appreciation of diversity leads to more collaborative international relationships, facilitating the sharing of ideas, solutions, and cultural treasures that enrich all nations involved.

Embracing your personal truth and walking the path of authenticity is a journey of self-discovery and a courageous act that influences others around you. By living authentically, you cultivate a sense of integrity and alignment in your life, leading to greater peace and satisfaction. This authenticity acts as a beacon, inspiring others to seek truth in their own lives.

As each person embraces their genuine self, the collective fabric of society becomes enriched with diversity and sincerity. The ripples of this authenticity can extend far, touching the lives of others in ways unseen, promoting a broader societal transformation toward truthfulness and transparency.

The decision to live truthfully requires courage, as it often involves stepping away from societal expectations and norms. It is about listening to your inner voice and honoring your true desires and beliefs, even when they go against the grain. This can lead to profound personal growth and resilience, as navigating life based on your true self equips you with the strength to face challenges confidently and gracefully. Moreover, this journey fosters a deep self-awareness that guides life's complexities, helping you make choices that are not only right for you but also inherently more fulfilling.

In essence, embracing the path of authenticity is a powerful choice that benefits yourself and the world around you. It encourages a life of purpose and joy, underscored by the light of your truth.

As you continue to honor your path, remember that your authenticity is a gift to the world, shining brightly and encouraging others to live their truth. Embrace this journey with open arms and an open heart, and watch as the world opens up in return.

By steadfastly adhering to your true self, you contribute to a more honest and open world, paving the way for future generations to embrace their authenticity. To inspire this journey, consider this quote:

"Be yourself; everyone else is already taken."

-Oscar Wilde.